Christmastime
in Montana

Christmastime
in Montana

Compiled by

Dave Walter

Montana Historical Society Press

Helena, Montana

Photo on page ii: Maurice Hain, grandson of Montana pioneer Granville Stuart, Christmas 1936; page vi: Dillon's Thelma Riley on her sled, 1905; page viii: Montana artist Leonard Lopp, Somers. All from the Montana Historical Society Photograph Archives, Helena

Book design and composition by Diane Gleba Hall
Typeset in Bodoni and Franklin Gothic
Printed by Thomson-Shore

Distributed by the Globe Pequot Press,
246 Goose Lane, Guilford, Connecticut 06437, (800) 243-0495

04 05 06 07 08 09 10   11 10 9 8 7 6 5 4 3 2

ISBN 0-917298-99-3

Library of Congress Cataloging-in-Publication Data
Christmastime in Montana / compiled by Dave Walter.— Rev. ed.
    p. cm.
ISBN 0-917298-99-3 (pbk. : alk. paper)
    1. Christmas—Montana—History. 2. Montana—Social life and customs.
    I. Walter, David, 1943–
GT4986.M9C48 2003
394.2663'09786—dc21

                                    2003013768

There can only be one choice here:

This work is dedicated to my parents,

Dorothy and George Walter,

who never gave up on me.

Contents

Illustrations

Acknowledgements

To the John and Mary Blair family, who live a few miles south of Swan Lake on Montana Highway 83, I am indebted for the idea for this book. I was driving to the Flathead Valley one evening in 1988, a few days before Christmas, to pick up my daughters, Emily and Amanda, for their Christmas vacation in Helena. The Seeley-Swan road had turned particularly slick and had become lined with an increasing number of deer, all adept at feints across the roadway. Dark had fallen before five o'clock, and the tall, dense forest seemed to intensify the night. Then, somewhere north of Lion Creek, it began to snow heavily, cutting the visibility even more. Slowed to what seemed a crawl, I finally reached a stretch of rebuilt highway leading into the town of Swan Lake.

Abruptly, out of the snowy, forested night loomed alongside the road a fifty-foot evergreen decked in brilliant, multicolored Christmas lights. The sight was a shock and a revelation. The huge tree was more welcomed than tire tracks in the snow. No symbol of the "spirit of Christmas" could have been more apt. As I steered slowly under the tree, it became a timeless

Skier at the entrance to Norris Geyser Basin in Yellowstone National Park, January 1887. F. Jay Haynes, photographer, Haynes Foundation Collection, Montana Historical Society Photograph Archives, Helena

reminder of all of the Christmases celebrated in Montana—the very essence of a Montana Christmas. And there the idea for this book was born. I am grateful for the Blair family's public expression of their Christmas spirit—then and now.

To Barbie Stahl Pelan, formerly of the Fords Creek Hutterite Colony, I am deeply indebted for her willingness to share her summary of a Hutterite Christmas. Moreover, she subsequently wrote a short autobiographical sketch—if anything, the more difficult task. Ms. Pelan's well-written, candid description is a rare glimpse into a lifestyle about which noncolonists need greater understanding. She remains kind, gracious, and thoughtful beyond her years.

Christmastime
in Montana

Introduction

*W*E REALLY have not been at this very long. The birth of the Christ child has been celebrated in Montana for fewer than two hundred years. Yet this particular holiday has developed into our major annual festival day, gathering momentum after Thanksgiving and dissolving into the more secular activities of New Year's Day. However removed we were—and are—from the American mainstream, Montanans have always found a way to create a feast, or to gather for a community observance, or to treasure the meaning of Christmas Day. Through these decades, Christmas has remained not only the greatest of children's holidays but also a time for adults to mix revelry with enactments of Christ's message of "Peace on earth; good will toward men."

Christmas in Montana, as everywhere in Christendom, then becomes a benchmark—a signpost we use to measure our time and reflect on our past and present accomplishments and disappointments. It provides the opportunity to stand back from the chaos and furor of daily life to consider some higher ideals and to assess our ability to live by those loftier standards during the rest of the year. This holiday—which strangely entwines the passage of the winter solstice, the birth of Christ to the Virgin Mary in a stable, and the tradition of Saint Nicholas in the guise of Santa Claus—evokes intensified emotions in each of us.

Reverend Job H. Little with the Neihart pastor's horse and conveyance. Montana Historical Society Photograph Archives, Helena

For these reasons, Christmas forms a useful slice of time to cut from our past and to peel apart, layer by layer. Those layers reveal both constants (tricky themes that seem to change, but do not) and evolving patterns in family and community customs. This compilation of pieces from our past is not merely a thick, fancy greeting card. This is a history book of sorts, for there are patterns at work in the Christmases of our past.

Look back through time at Montana Christmases not to discover the components of an "old-fashioned Christmas." Find instead developing patterns of celebration—patterns that continue to evolve, subject to myriad factors. Look at Christmas as a useful mechanism to cut through Montana history and to lay bare some of the social and cultural practices of Montanans. Look at Christmas in Montana to learn about our lives, our feelings for each other, and our relationships with the Montana land. The patterns are there.

With apologies to Bing Crosby, the term "white Christmas" aptly can be applied to Montana. For this Christian festival day comes to Montana with the earliest explorers, fur trappers, missionaries, and settlers as an element of white civilization, for which the resident Native Americans held no context. Native bands had developed their own customs of gift-giving, which extended throughout the year and were not tied to a single, annual event. To many Native Americans, the observance of Christmas became little more than a double-barrelled attempt to "Christianize and civilize" at the expense of native culture. As the fur trader Ross Cox discovered at Saleesh House in 1813, the native must embrace Christianity before he can properly celebrate the birth of Christ. On some of Montana's reservations, Christmas remains essentially a white holiday.

The white prospectors and settlers drawn to Montana's placer gold strikes in the 1860s brought Christmas as an element of their heritage, although they came from diverse European and American backgrounds. Mining camp Christmases first proved quite raucous—really little more than annual excuses for extended drunks. Not uncommonly, alcohol led to violence on the Montana frontier. With the arrival of families (particularly women and children), however, "cultured" alternatives for the holidays quickly surfaced. By the 1870s, whether a town could observe Christmas without excessive public drunkenness and open violence became a measure of its cultural sophistication.

Other patterns rapidly developed in the celebration of Montana Christmases. The Sunday School Christmas-tree presentation served as the prime Christmas event in an age when few families decorated trees in their own homes. Usually held on Christmas Eve, this occasion often included the minister preaching a short sermon, the Sunday School classes singing carols, and individual children reciting memorized Christmas verses and stories. Although not so prominent as he later would become, Santa Claus then appeared to distribute gifts. These parcels had been placed on the boughs of the sect's candle-lit tree, and they frequently contained oranges, apples, nuts, and hard candy.

The people of Butte attempted to hold a non-sectarian, community Christmas-tree event in 1876, but it proved a dismal failure. Church Christmas-tree presentations survived well into the twentieth century, particularly in rural churches and among ethnic congregations. Similarly, the traditional parcel of apples, oranges, nuts, and hard candy was given to children at least through the Depression.

The move to community-wide, secular Christmas exercises generally began in Montana after 1910, and these celebrations survive today in some of the state's smaller towns. At about the same time, many Christmas programs moved out of the churches and into the public schools—often because the homesteaders' one-room schoolhouse served as the area's largest meeting hall. Particularly during crises (such as World War I, periods of widespread drought, the Depression, and World War II), these school programs became rallying points and statements of a community's determination to survive by preserving its Christmas traditions.

As much as a Montana Christmas has been the occasion for the gathering of family and friends, it also has become a focused occasion to provide for the needy among us. Through much of the nineteenth century, this type of Christmas giving was practiced on an individual basis. Then, around the turn of the century, private social-welfare and fraternal groups organized to care for the children and the poor families in Montana's larger towns.

While some of these private-sector programs survive to the present, others have been absorbed by federal and state welfare-agency operations. The constant element in this pattern is the individual who quietly takes on a

Christmas project and maintains it year after year—like Billy Gemmell and the Joshers' Club in Butte, or "Daddy" Reeves and his annual portrayal of Santa through five decades, or the Harriet Theatre children's programs in Hardin, or Helena's "Secret Santa" in the 1980s.

Montanans also have observed the Christmas holiday with changing tastes in decorating. The adornment of business establishments began with sidewalk displays by butcher shops in the 1860s. Then, just before World War I, commercial decorating burgeoned with interior and window displays. This trend developed into exterior business decorations after the Depression. Tied to the realization that the Christmas buying season had become the major component of the sales year, Chambers of Commerce and commercial groups promoted local Christmas events. These activities included the seasonal "arrival of Santa Claus" and the decoration of the town's business district— a responsibility more recently relegated to the municipal governments in many Montana towns.

Yet Montanans have relied more on civic and social groups than on businesses to define their Christmas festivities. Projects like the toy-repair program in Stanford, the community Christmas tree in Denton, and the Meaderville Volunteer Fire Department's elaborate holiday displays have proven crucial elements of each town's Christmas tradition. With the general availability of electricity, the increase in disposable income, and the decline in community-wide activities, decorating the exteriors of private homes became a prevalent Christmas practice throughout Montana after World War II.

Yet, for all the changing rituals in Montana's past Christmases, there exist some real constants in our holiday pageantry. And these basic practices seem subject to little variation. Despite the charge (first levelled during the Victorian era) that "Christmas has become too commercialized," Montanans regularly have marked the holiday season in time-honored ways: members of the rural women's club exchange small gifts at their December meeting; Sunday School classes carol through the neighborhood and at the local hospital; military personnel pass a lonely Christmas far from home; townspeople contribute to the Salvation Army's red kettles to provide Christmas necessities for poor families; Montana turkey ranchers and Christmas-tree farmers harvest their crops for national distribution; young men and women return from out-of-town jobs and schools to spend the holidays with their families; mothers and hotel chefs prepare and serve their finest dishes.

Montana's Christmas celebrations continue to evolve, overlapping and blending the older customs with the newer practices. As times and circumstances change—through economic depressions, wars, and personal tragedies—the Christmas holiday remains an anchor to which each Montanan ties his or her life.

To each of us, "Christmastime in Montana" evokes myriad images—childhood delights and disappointments, thoughtful giving to the less fortunate, strong emotions tied to family and friends, and gratitude for the opportunity to spend another year in Montana's often breathtaking surroundings. It also provides an occasion for us to remove ourselves somewhat from the mundane and to reflect on the "spirit of Christmas." In this context, the birth of Christ prompts thoughts of love for one's fellow human, of the tolerance of others' practices and beliefs, of the exercise of charity toward the needy, and of thanksgiving for trusting friends and a rewarding life.

In this vein, Montana newspapers long have honored the American journalistic tradition of presenting the "Christmas editorial." Such writings engaged in just this sort of removed, reflective observation. In addition to their annual Christmas wish of "Peace on earth, good will toward men," many Montana editors have decried our inability to live the rest of the year by these Christmas, Christian precepts. Of course they are correct; we need to try harder.

At its best, a historical look at the celebration of Christmas in Montana will evoke in each of us memories of bygone Christmases. For, while the holiday is a constant in the passage of our lives, how we choose to observe Christmas Day has changed considerably. Only one percent of Americans report having eaten plum pudding last Christmas; for every American home that had a real Christmas tree last year, another home erected and decorated an artificial tree. Christmas practices continue in flux.

During this holiday season, Montanans might benefit from a look at this slice of our history—"Christmases past," as well as "Christmas present." For almost two centuries we annually have celebrated this one, fine, sacred event. The nature of those celebrations tells us more about who we Montanans are than do most other slices of Montana history.

Exploration and Fur Trade

*W*HITE EXPLORERS, travelers, fur trappers, and fur traders brought the earliest vestiges of Christmastime to what would become Montana. As these whites probed the intricate social networks of native societies, spread across a broad Montana landscape, they carried their cultural inheritances with them. And Christmas was a piece—an important piece—of that culture. Yet Montana natives already practiced their own series of winter-solstice observances, so the white visitors simply laid Christian observances and rites atop a rich stratum of native winter ceremonies and storytelling.

Christmas to many of these displaced whites offered an opportunity to remember and to mark elements of their familial and cultural pasts. In turn those remembrances infused the Christmas practices of many immigrant Montanans through the centuries. Christmas still provides a chance to look back as well as to count current blessings. It served the same purpose for the earliest white Montanans.

Free Trappers, by Charles M. Russell (oil on canvas, 1911). Montana Historical Society Museum, Helena

A Fur Trader's Christmas, 1813

Ross Cox was an Irishman who came to the Northwest in 1812 as an employee of John Jacob Astor's Pacific Fur Company. When that company sold its assets in 1813, Cox transferred his allegiance to the North West Company. In November 1813, he was ordered from Spokane House to join James McMillan at Saleesh House, where they would conduct the winter trade with local Salish bands.

Saleesh House had been constructed by David Thompson of the North West Company in 1809. It was located just a bit upstream from the present-day town of Thompson Falls, on the north bank of the Clark Fork River.

The Trapper, by Charles M. Russell (pen and ink, 1901). Mackay Collection, Montana Historical Society Museum, Helena

*W*E ARRIVED SAFELY at Spokan House, at which place I slept one night [November 21, 1813], and then continued on for the Flat-heads with eight men and twelve loaded horses. We pursued the same route I had followed the preceding winter with my friend [Russell] Farnham, through the thick woods along the banks of the Flathead River. After suffering great hardships from cold and snow, we reached Mr. [James] McMillan on the 24th of December, with the loss of two horses, which we were obliged to leave in the woods from exhaustion.

The fort was about forty miles higher up in an easterly direction than the place Farnham and I had chosen for the log-house. It had a good trading store, a comfortable house for the men, and a snug box for ourselves—all situated on a point formed by the junction of a bold mountain torrent with the Flat-head River, and surrounded on all sides with high and thickly wooded hills, covered with pine, spruce, larch, beech, birch, and cedar.

A large band of the Flat-head warriors were encamped about the fort. They had recently returned from the buffalo country, and had revenged their defeat of the preceding year by a signal victory over their enemies the Black-feet, several of whose warriors, with their women, they had taken prisoner. McMillan's tobacco and stock of trading goods had been entirely expended previous to my arrival, and the Indians were much in want of ammunition, etc. My appearance (or I should rather say, the goods I brought with me) was therefore a source of great joy to both parties. The natives smoked the much-loved weed for several days successively.

Our hunters killed a few mountain sheep, and I brought up a bag of flour, a bag of rice, plenty of tea and coffee, some arrowroot, and fifteen gallons of prime rum. We spent a comparatively happy Christmas and, by the side of a blazing fire in a warm room, forgot the sufferings we endured in our dreary progress through the woods.

There was, however, in the midst of our festivities, a great drawback from the pleasure we should otherwise have enjoyed. I allude to the unfortunate Black-feet who had been captured by the Flat-heads. Having been informed that they were about putting one of their prisoners to death, I went to their camp to witness the spectacle.

We remonstrated to the Flat-heads against the exercise of such horrible cruelties. They replied by saying the Black-feet treated their relations in the same manner; that it was the course adopted by all red warriors; and that they could not think of giving up the gratification of their revenge to the foolish and womanish feelings of white men.

We renewed our remonstrances, but received nearly the same answer as before. Finding them still inflexible, and wishing to adopt every means in our power, consistent with safety, in the cause of humanity, we ordered our interpreter to acquaint them that, highly as we valued their friendship, and much as we esteemed their furs, we would quit their country forever unless they discontinued their unmanly and disgraceful cruelties to their prisoners.

We told them that this act of self-denial on their part was peculiarly grateful to the white men; and that by it they would secure our permanent residence among them and, in return for their furs, be always furnished with guns and ammunition sufficient to repel the attacks of their old enemies, and preserve their relations from being made prisoners. This decided the doubtful; and the chief promised faithfully that no more tortures should be inflicted on the prisoners, which I believe was rigidly adhered to, at least for that winter.

Ross Cox, *Adventures on the Columbia River* (New York, 1832)

John Work at Flathead Post, 1825

John Work came from Ireland to the Hudson's Bay area in 1814, as a clerk for the Hudson's Bay Company. He was reassigned to the Pacific Northwest as a trader in 1821 when the Hudson's Bay Company merged with the North West Company. Work operated out of Spokane House, making winter trading trips into the Flathead country in both 1824 and 1825. In the latter year, he wintered over at the Hudson's Bay Company's Flathead Post, situated just upstream from Eddy, on the Clark Fork River in Sanders County. John Work later became the leader of several large fur brigades that explored and traded throughout the West.

*D*ECEMBER 25, 1825: Cloudy, Raw, cold weather. Masses of ice running pretty thick down the River.—This being Christmas Day the two men here had a dram, and we served out each an extra ration of fresh meat, a tongue, and a quart of Flour. For the old freeman Bastang, the same.

> T. C. Elliott, ed., "Journal of John Work,
> December 15, 1825, to June 12, 1825" *Washington
> Historical Quarterly*, 5 (October 1914): 263

Father de Smet at St. Mary's, 1841

The Montana Salish dispatched four separate Indian delegations to St. Louis during the 1830s to attract the Jesuit "Black Robes" west. Finally, in 1841, Father Pierre-Jean de Smet, two other priests, and three lay brothers arrived in the Bitterroot Valley. They began immediately to construct St. Mary's Mission at present-day Stevensville. This religious outpost served the region's natives until 1850.

Father de Smet traveled extensively in the West during the 1840s, 1850s, and 1860s—alternating trips up the Missouri River with voyages to Europe to raise funds for his missionary work. This remarkable, dedicated pioneer also found the time to keep wonderfully descriptive journals of his experiences. He died in 1873, at the age of seventy-two.

ON MY RETURN [to St. Mary's Mission], on the 8th of December, I continued instructing those of the Flatheads who had not been baptized. On Christmas Day I added 150 new baptisms to those [60 baptisms at Horse Prairie] of the 3d of December, and thirty-two rehabilitations of marriage; so that the Flatheads, some sooner and others later, but all, with very few exceptions, had, in the space of three months, complied with everything necessary to merit the glorious title of true children of God.

Accordingly, on Christmas Eve, a few hours before the midnight mass, the village of St. Mary was deemed worthy of a special mark of heaven's favor. The Blessed Virgin appeared to a little orphan boy named Paul, in the hut of an aged and truly pious woman. The youth, piety, and sincerity of this child, joined to the nature of the fact which he related, forbade us to doubt the truth of his statement. The following is what he recounted to me with his own innocent lips:

"Upon entering John's hut, whither I had gone to learn my prayers, which I did not know, I saw some one who was very beautiful—her feet did not touch the earth, her garments were as white as snow; she had a star over her head, a serpent under her feet; and near the serpent was a fruit which I did not recognize. I could see her heart, from which rays of light burst forth and shone upon me. When I first beheld all this, I was frightened but afterward my fear left me; my heart was warmed, my mind clear, and I do not know how it happened, but all at once I knew my prayers."

He ended his account by saying that several times the same person had appeared to him whilst he was sleeping; and that once she had told him she was pleased that the first village of the Flatheads should be called

Father Pierre-Jean de Smet, circa 1863. Gustavus Sohon, photographer, Montana Historical Society Photograph Archives, Helena

"St. Mary." The child had never seen or heard before anything of the kind; he did not even know if the person was a man or woman, because the appearance of the dress which she wore was entirely unknown to him. Several persons having interrogated the child on this subject, have found him unvarying in his answers. He continues by his conduct to be the angel of his tribe.

Hiram M. Chittenden and Alfred T. Richardson,
Life, Letters and Travels of
Father Pierre-Jean DeSmet, S.J.,
vol. 1 (New York, 1905)

Christmas at Fort Lewis, 1850

Lieutenant James H. Bradley served in Montana Territory with the United States Army during the 1860s and 1870s. While stationed at Fort Benton, he was inspired by local fur-trade men to record the history of the fur industry and military campaigns in the Upper Missouri. In this selection, Bradley recounts the naming of Fort Benton in 1850 by Alexander Culbertson, the Upper Missouri Outfit's regional superintendent from 1840 through the late 1850s. Culbertson was renowned in the Missouri River fur trade for his intelligence, energy, fidelity, and close, ethical ties with the area's natives. Lieutenant Bradley was killed fighting the Nez Perce in the Battle of the Big Hole on August 9, 1877.

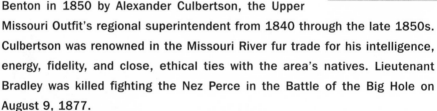

*T*HE FALL was an unusually open one, warm weather continuing until late in December, and Major Culbertson resolved to improve it by the inauguration of his long-contemplated plan of rebuilding his post [Fort Lewis] in adobe. The soil of the bottom was found excellently adapted to the manufacture of the brick, and the work was pushed with vigor. Day by day the walls

St. Ignatius Mission, by Peter Toftt (watercolor on paper, circa 1865). Montana Historical Society Museum, Helena

of his two-story dwelling rose higher and higher, on the site of a former log building taken down to make room for it.

Toward the last, the nights began to be cold, and the adobes froze. But, as the best that could be done, they were laid in the walls yet unhardened, where fortunately they dried without any cracking or weakening of the walls. Just before Christmas, the building was completed.

On Christmas night, it was dedicated by a big ball. Until a late hour, the light-headed voyageurs and their squaw wives, sweethearts, and friends danced and whirled to the music of several fiddles. In the midst of the festivities, Major Culbertson proposed that, in consideration of the warm friendship of Senator Thomas H. Benton for the partners of the American Fur Company, and his services in saving the Company from ruin in 1844 by effecting a compromise of the suit brought against it, that the post should be re-named in his honor.

The proposition was received with acclamation by the joyous assembly and thus upon Christmas night, 1850, the post was first called by the name it still bears and that will probably ever distinguish the locality—Fort Benton.

"Affairs at Fort Benton," Manuscript
Collection 49, James H. Bradley Papers,
Montana Historical Society Archives, Helena

Fort Owen Journals, 1854–1867

John Owen arrived in western Montana in 1849. In 1850 he purchased the St. Mary's Mission complex (near present-day Stevensville) from the Jesuit fathers, who had determined to move to a location more suited to their missionary efforts. Owen quickly gained the confidence of local Salish bands, and he operated as a free trader from the post between 1850 and 1872. During this time he created a diverse commercial operation at the site, including an expanded farming program and a highly productive grist mill.

Owen's hospitality became legendary on the frontier, and his fairness as a trader brought him great financial success. This Bitterroot pioneer witnessed the early settlement of the valley by whites, and he recorded that development for two decades.

John Owen returned to Philadelphia in 1877, and he died in the East in 1899—all but forgotten in the burgeoning state he had pioneered.

*F*RIDAY, DECEMBER 22, 1854: Mr. Burr and Mr. Ogden's party arrived from above.

Saturday, December 3, 1854: Snake Indians arrived.

Monday, December 25, 1854: Mr. Burr's Snake Wife left.

Sunday, December 31, 1854: Christmas is over and gone, and the year too. We had quite a Merry time. Mince Pies and Cakes that would have done Credit to a table in a More Civilized part of the World. There was but one thing to Mar our pleasure and that was the departure of Mr. Burr's Wife, who left his bed and board without just and Sufficient provocation. She was visited by her parents on the 23rd and when they left she took the opportunity of going also. Most of the past Month the weather has been quite unpleasant—Not on account of the Severity of the Cold or Snow but the general Blusterytime.

Friday, December 21, 1855: Mesrs. Harris and Adams returned, finding the Snow too deep in Hell's Gate defile and the Weather too Severe for travelling.

Tuesday, December 25, 1855: [no entry]

Monday, December 31, 1855: Mr. Adams and Judge Barr gone out hunting. Another Year has Closed upon us. The last ten days the Weather has been quite Severe, but at present has the appearance of Moderating. We had a pleasant Christmas, with Some of the good things of this World—Sufficient Brandy for Punches and Mince Pies, which were got up in very good Style, at least we all thought So from the demonstrations Made when the Cook placed them before us at dinner. We unexpectedly had the pleasure of Mesrs. Harris and Adams to pass the Christmas with us, they being Compelled to return from their trip to Beaver Head.

Thursday, December 24, 1857: Mr. Ogden and Mr. Adams rode up from Hells Gate and Mr. Burr from above, for the purpose of passing the Christmas.

Friday, December 25, 1857: Christmas is past and gone.—The day passed off quietly and very pleasantly. Mr. Chase and Mr. Harris got up a Very Nice Egg Nog in the Morning and, as for the dinner, few in a More civilized World can boast of a better one.

Sunday, December 27, 1857: Mesrs. Burr, Adams, and Ogden left for their respective homes.

Monday, December 24, 1860: Mr. Adams and Mr. Stewart rode down from above. Party also arrived from Hells Gate to pass Christmas.

Tuesday, December 25, 1860: Bright and Cold. Passed a very pleasant day. Had a dance at Night. The Young Misses Grant, Mrs. Miller, and Mrs. Van Ettan in fact all Enjoyed themselves.

Wednesday, December 24, 1862: Butchered a Young Steer I had purchased of old Chief Victor. Mr. Harris also Butchered another fine Mutton. Preparations are going on for a family ("Christmas") dinner on Tomorrow, Mrs. Harris sent Me a few doz. Eggs for Tomorrow. The party will certainly toast her with well filled Goblets. The Key of a Small family house I have had built Was turned over to Me to day. A flagon of grog issued on the occasion.

Thursday, December 25, 1862: The Christmas passed off as usual. Calls, Salutes of Small Arms, Egg Nogg, etc. etc. Mr. Harris last Night gave us a Salute from the four-lb. Brass Howitzer. Mr. Banty and Lady, Mr. Peters and Lady Called and took dinner with us, and the day wound up with a dance.

Saturday, December 24, 1864: [Entry logged by Thomas W. Harris, John Owen's assistant.] This is a very dull Christmas Eve. I took three drinks before supper to the memory of my old friend Maj. Owen, who is absent, which made me feel quite lively, in fact almost too tite. I never missed any one so much as I do the Maj. Owen, who has now been absent from home over thirteen months. Report is that he has been killed by the Indians, but I don't believe it.

Sunday, December 25, 1864: This has been rather a dull Christmas, although we had an Egg nog this morning, besides Sundry drinks of good Brandy during the day and this evening. My wife gave us a very good Supper. Maj. Graham, Mr. Johnson, Chatfield, Mr. Roberts, and my Brother were present.

Sunday, December 24, 1865: The Bros. Harris in from Three Mile Creek.—Rode up to Stevensville With them and imbibed a couple drinks of "Bourbon Syrup." Mr. Pattee returned to Missoula; His Bride Not being Well, remained at her Brothers'.—Things look dull for Christmas.—Well, we can Say that the Mill Warming and Wedding was Sufficient for the day thereof.

Monday, December 25, 1865: The Most quiet Christmas I have Ever Seen at Fort Owen.—Last Night Mr. Chatfield fired a Salute from the Mountain Howitzer, which has been about all the demonstrating Made—Excepting the health and happiness of friends far away was drank by all hands.— Received an Eastern Mail; also 400 feet in two Rich Lodes.

Tuesday, December 26, 1865: The Bros. Harris in from 3 Mile Creek.— Had an Oyster Supper at Mr. Lou Harris's Store. Enjoyed it hugely.

Saturday, December 22, 1866: George ran the Mill all last Night. He has ground Some 200 Bu. Wheat Since Breakfast Yesterday. Not an Ice cicle on the flume. Such Weather for Mid-Winter.

Monday, December 24, 1866: George ran the Mill until Midnight last Night on the General's Grist. Turned the Water out of the flume.

Tuesday, December 25, 1866: Cloudy and Snowing. Mr. Dobbins and Mr. Cone down and passed the Evening. Mr. F.B.O. brewed a *Very* Nice Egg Nogg.

Wednesday, December 26, 1866: No one Stirring Much.

Tuesday, December 24, 1867: Another Willamette Morning. Rainy with Warm South Wind. Started the Wheel. Intend running the Mill Tonight.

Wednesday, December 25, 1867: Ran Mill until 4 O'clock this Morning on toll Wheat. Mill busy all day. We have Spent our Christmas in the Mill, while friends in a distant land were spending theirs in the good old Way. My Cook gave us a Very Nice dinner. Roast chickens—took the place of Turkey. We had Nice Mince pies—Cakes—Tarts and Dough Nutes. All of Which was relished hugely. Had No Strangers to dinner. It has been Soft and Cloudy the Entire day. Received Mail.

Thursday, December 26, 1867: Mill busy all day and running finely. The Wind South all day and thawing. Mill about clear of Wheat.

"Fort Owen Journals,"
Manuscript Collection 44, John Owen Papers,
Montana Historical Society Archives, Helena

Granville Stuart's First Christmas in Montana, 1857

The Stuart brothers—James (1832–1873) and Granville (1834–1918)—arrived in the Deer Lodge Valley in 1857 from California, via Utah. In 1858 Granville discovered gold in the American Fork area, foreshadowing the Montana gold rushes of the 1860s. During the succeeding decades, the prospector became a mercantiler, a freighter, a banker, a librarian, a stockman, a foreign ambassador, and a legislator. *Forty Years on the Frontier*, his autobiographical account of his Montana exploits, remains a classic western book.

In contrast to Owen's account, Stuart's narrative suggests the growing western influence on Christmas feasts.

M y first Christmas dinner in Montana was eaten in the year 1857, a little below Melrose. In that year there were few white men in this part of the country. I was camped on the Big Hole River, just above the "Backbone." In company with my brother James, Reece Anderson, and Jacob Weeks, I lived in an Indian skin lodge. It was about the time of the Mountain Meadow Massacre. There was a state of warfare between the Mormons and the United States government in Utah, and to the north we saw our only safe exit.

Granville Stuart, 1883. L. A. Huffman, photographer, Montana Historical Society Photograph Archives, Helena

We crossed the divide into what is now Montana on the 14th day of October, 1857, and we remained in the vicinity of Dillon's location until the last of that November, when we set up camp on that spot below Melrose. The cattle that we had bought from Captain Richard Grant were footsore and poor. We turned them out, not even surmising what the coming winter might do to them.

But there was no winter! In October a thick cake of ice covered the Big Hole River, but in midwinter the river broke up, and there was no more ice. There was a light snowfall in the following January [1858]. Aside from this, it was a dry and dusty winter. The cattle came out in the spring fat enough for beef, but as game was abundant we did not have to kill them.

On Christmas Day, I took my gun and went out after a mountain sheep. I got a young one, and before I reached camp I thought it was full-grown, for it was very heavy when I got there. I wore no coat—the forenoon bright and fair. In the afternoon I went up the river about a mile to a warm spring that we had discovered earlier. I banked up a pool of water and took a bath under a clear sky. But, before I was dressed, a sharp wind from the northwest came up, and I nearly froze to death.

Our menu was, on that day: roast mountain mutton, black coffee, and sourdough bread. We had no vegetables all that winter. And later we had a long siege of eating nothing but meat.

Anaconda Standard, December 17, 1899

Gold Discoveries and Settlement

W HILE THE FUR TRADE enticed only a trickle of whites to what would become Montana, the discovery of placer gold at Bannack in 1862 opened the floodgates of immigration. Miners and prospectors chased the elusive gold into western and central Montana through the 1870s, building roughhewn mining camps that became settlements if they could justify their existence after the mother lodes played out.

When women and children arrived in these frontier communities, Christmas gained real legitimacy. From an all-male excuse for a days-long drunk, it evolved into a reflection of the settlers' eastern, Christian roots. Although limited by isolation and a scattered populace, Christmas took on celebratory elements easily recognizable throughout "the States."

At Home in My Cabin on Elk Creek, Montana Territory, by Peter Toftt (watercolor on paper, 1866). Montana Historical Society Museum, Helena

Christmas in Bannack, 1863

Martha Edgerton Plassman was a daughter of the first Territorial Governor of Montana, Sidney Edgerton. The family came to Bannack in 1863 when Martha was 13 years old. The placer-gold strike had occurred at Bannack in July of 1862—the first of scores of discoveries that would draw whites into the Montana wilderness. Martha's adult life was spent as a teacher, author, and editor, in addition to raising seven children alone after the death of her husband. She died in Great Falls in 1936.

"Give the child one well-selected book every Christmas, and all his life he will thank you."

I speak with some experience on this subject. My father was a book-lover. He saw to it that every birthday and Christmas should be made memorable for his children with books. I came to expect them on these occasions, and I shall never forget my aggrieved feeling when my thirteenth Christmas saw no book.

We were then living in Bannack City. It was in Idaho Territory for that Christmas, but was in Montana Territory on the next one. It was 1863, and books in that little mining camp were not regarded as one of the necessities of life. There was no book store and no library. What books had found their way across the Plains had passed from hand to hand. They were read from cover to cover at least once and, in numerous cases, they were read many times each.

On Christmas Day, the weather was intensely cold; the ground was covered with snow. We children

General View of Marysville and adjacent Quarts Mills near Bannack, Montana, by Peter Toftt (watercolor on paper, 1866). Montana Historical Society Museum, Helena

had hung our stockings near the stone fire place. But Santa Claus did not bring the usual gifts to Bannack.

In place of a book on that notable Christmas morning, I received a pair of stout shoes. There was nothing fancy about them, not even copper tips— at that time a feature much worn by children. It goes without saying that I was in sore need of new shoes. For those that I had worn from Ohio were in a sad condition, from three months of tramping through mud, sagebrush, and sand, from climbing mountains, from wading streams, and from treading rocky ways. Yes, there was no doubt that I needed them and that they cost a good

round sum in gold. But I hated them! That Christmas was no Christmas for me, for it was one without a book.

Montana Newspaper Association
Insert series, December 13, 1926

Wilbur Fisk Sanders, Virginia City, 1863

In September of 1863, Wilbur Fisk Sanders (1834–1905) and his uncle, Sidney Edgerton, arrived in Bannack. Within months, Sanders's legal acumen and personal bravery made him the Vigilantes' prosecuting attorney. He subsequently became a creator of Montana Territory's legal system and a strong Republican politician. He served in the Territorial Legislature (1873–1879) and received the Republican appointment to the United States Senate (1890–1893). Just prior to his death, the Montana Legislature recognized the contributions of this pioneer with the designation of Sanders County in western Montana.

CHRISTMAS DAY, 1863, was spent by me at Virginia City. Four nights before, the good citizens of the gulch had hanged a murderer, George Ives, with resolute sternness, resolving to put an end to a saturnalia of robbery and blood. Because the brunt of that prosecution fell into my hands and was pushed with a prudent but remorseless vigor, the animosity of Ives' accomplices was directed more particularly toward me—although there were others who also were marked for slaughter. The miners, mechanics, teamsters, and merchants who had stayed by that trial and remained until it culminated in the death of the victim, in the apprehension that I was in mortal peril, selected for me a bodyguard of four persons to remain with me night and day. I was thenceforth, for five or six days, to form an intimate acquaintance with Michael Tovey, Sr., Conrad Weary, and two or three other gentlemen.

Our turkeys came from the Salt Lake Valley and cost from $25 to $40 apiece. Our Christmas dinner was at the "Mechanical Bakery" late in the day, and meanwhile we discharged the not-entirely-customary social functions. My own memory of them clusters principally around the "Kiskaddon

[Christmastime in Montana]

Building." Here Billy Rumsey and the other members of the firm of Taylor, Thompson and Company (in modest and temperate spirit) dispensed a "nog" concocted of fresh eggs and other ingredients of spirits and species selected by that prince of caterers, Mr. Barnum.

I remark in passing that the adjective "fresh," as used above, is a relative term and that the eggs were imported from Salt Lake City and not from "the States." This distinction even now should be deemed important, as it was then the line of demarkation between the aristocracy and the common herd. I recall that John A. Creighton, that prince of good fellows, complained of the staleness of Barnum's eggs and produced some which he said were homemade and fresh from "the States," from which he fabricated another "nog" of very palatable quality.

The existing conditions had impelled us to form a Vigilance Committee, then in its chrysalis state, and we watched each other with intense solicitude, wondering if (in the crisis certain to come) there would be any flinching. Considering that we were strangers each to the others, and that some strained relations resulting from the Civil War existed, and that we were isolated from home beyond the conception of those not there—we, nevertheless, had a good cheer and voted that we had enjoyed a very Merry Christmas.

Anaconda Standard, December 17, 1899

Christmas Notices from Virginia City, 1864

*W*E NOTICE at Williams & Russell's meat market, a large lot of ducks and other specimens of the feathered tribes—just the thing for a Christmas dinner. Go early and secure one ere they are all gone.

CHRISTMAS CHEER.—The folks at the Star Restaurant are preparing for Christmas. A game dinner, with puddings, pies and old style fixings will be ready for their friends. Call there and try their skill.

Virginia City Montana Post, December 24, 1864.

Bear Meat and Frozen Onions, Virginia City, 1863

William Thompson came to Virginia City in 1863 from Dakota Territory, where he had apprenticed as a carpenter. He worked in the mining camp as a merchant and a lumberman before relocating to Glendale (1876) and then Butte (1879). Thompson served in both the House and the Senate of the Montana Legislative Assembly (1887–1891), and he was the mayor of Butte in the mid-1890s. This successful pioneer died in Butte in 1900 at the age of 62. His account of his first Christmas in Montana illustrates the importance of the traditional holiday to the mining camp's motley population—regardless of circumstances.

My first Christmas in Montana was spent at Virginia City in 1863. I was baching with my partner, Joe Griffith, and two other trail-blazers named Nunley and Clanton. We had come to this country over Lander's Cutoff to Oregon. Alder Gulch would be my home for 13 years.

In due time we started in to prepare a great feast for our first Christmas in the far West. A friend had sent us a piece of cinnamon-bear meat, and this my partner put into the oven and roasted. We had lots of flour, because we brought a supply with us; but vegetables were not to be had. I knew where there were some frozen onions behind a store. The onions had been frozen since the first cold spell of the season and had lain out in the backyard in a box with all kinds of trash. I think that I paid the storekeeper $3 for a couple of pounds of the frozen onions. I put them in a big iron pot and boiled them until we thought they must certainly be cooked.

The dinner was served. It consisted of bear meat, onions, salt-rising bread, cake, coffee, and sugar. Tom Clanton had been over at a saloon trying to win a gallon of whiskey for the feast, and his partner, Nunley, spent the forenoon rustling for the cake. He was acquainted with a family who gave him the privilege of their cookstove in which to bake a cake.

We sat down to the Christmas spread. Joe cut the bear and I dished up the onions; Nunley cut the cake and Clanton poured the booze. I scraped the onions on my plate to one side and settled down to enjoy the bear meat, which smelled so good while it was being cooked. Golly, but it was rank, tough, and stringy. I couldn't go it; I never could go whiskey; Nunley's cake was simply unapproachable. I filled up on coffee and bread. Joe ate the onions, but he only tasted the bear. The other boys filled up a little on everything in sight. Nunley ate all of the cake just to prove to us that it was really good. The next day he called in the medicine man.

Anaconda Standard, December 17, 1899

Gohn's Butcher Shop, Virginia City

The practice of decorating commercial establishments for the Christmas holidays began in Montana with butcher shops during the placer-mining period. The use of evergreens was particularly popular.

$\mathcal{G}$EORGE GOHN's butcher-shop, in our opinion, displayed the greatest variety of domestic and wild meats on Christmas Day. To an epicure, a mere

Highland City Meat Market and other Helena businesses viewed from the northwest corner of Main and Bridge Streets, circa 1869. Montana Historical Society Photograph Archives, Helena

view of the many "fat things, full of marrow" would have been worth the price
of an ordinary dinner.

Virginia City Montana Post, December 30, 1865

Father Giorda's Christmas Mass, 1865

Father Joseph Giorda, S. J., first conducted services in Virginia City in the fall of
1863, returning several times prior to the Christmas of 1865. The announced
meeting proved most successful, and the Virginia City Opera House was purchased with donated funds to become All Saints Catholic Church thereafter.
Acting Governor Thomas Francis Meagher died mysteriously in Fort Benton in
July of 1867.

*I*T IS THE most pleasant part of our chronicling labors to record the
advancement, in these wild and isolated mountains, of the cause of enlight-
ened religion and civilization. The Catholics—who are always found shoulder to shoulder with the very first of pioneers in disseminating the principles
of Christianity—are about to erect a church in Virginia City.

The Reverend Joseph Giorda of the Jesuit Fathers has arrived in town
from St. Peter's Mission, on the Missouri, for the purpose of ministering to the
spiritual wants of our Catholic fellow citizens of Virginia [City] and Nevada
[City] and to the other towns and mining settlements of the neighborhood during this Christmas season. He will celebrate High Mass on Christmas Eve at
12 o'clock in the United States courtroom, over Olinghouse's store; and also
on the Christmas Day, at the same place, at 10:30 o'clock in the morning.

Immediately after Mass on Christmas Day, a meeting of the Catholics of
this section will be held for the purpose of providing funds for the erection of
a church and the support of the clergyman. Acting-Governor Thomas F.
Meagher will preside. It is a matter in which general interest should be felt,
and we hope all, irrespective of creed, will bear a helping hand. Nothing more
elevates the social tone of frontier communities than the establishment of
organizations and the erection of temples of worship. Father Giorda will
remain in the city until the late spring.

Virginia City Montana Post, December 23, 1865

Interior of the First Episcopal Church in Virginia City, early 1870s. O. C. Bundy, photographer, Montana Historical Society Photograph Archives, Helena

The Children's Christmas, Helena, 1866

The first white immigrants to Montana's gold camps lived a fairly basic existence, yet they brought with them deep-seated traditions from varied cultures and from more sophisticated societies. Christmas offered these settlers an opportunity to transplant a bit of that culture in the Montana wilderness.

THE CHRISTMAS EVE exercises of the children of the Methodist Episcopal Sunday School was one of the finest occasions of its kind that has as yet taken place in the Territory. It is one, too, that reflected the very highest credit on all concerned. The old Theater building on Bridge Street was beautifully wreathed with evergreens, and the stage was adorned with a splendidly illuminated and beautifully provided Christmas tree.

The scholars were arranged on the stage, and the pit and the gallery were densely packed. There was a large attendance of the blushing maids and blooming matrons of Helena, who lent a charm and grace to the scene that reminded not a few people of other days and other climes.

The opening exercises were followed by the dialogues and the reading of fugitive pieces by the scholars, who acquitted themselves in an excellent manner. We cannot particularize when all of the presenters did so well.

After this came the distribution of the presents on the tree. Bright eyes shone brighter (even of those often of an adult age) as the presents of friends, and mayhap lovers, were handed to their owners. After the singing of the doxology, and a benediction by the Reverend A. M. Haugh, the assemblage dispersed—the little ones to revel in their present gifts and to dream of Santa Claus, and the older ones well-pleased with an entertainment that will be a green spot in their memory long days hence.

Virginia City Montana Post, December 29, 1866

Suicide in Argenta, Christmas 1866

Although Christmas is a time of joyous celebration for most, it frequently intensifies loneliness for some, separated from home and loved ones at this special time of year. This depression can lead to desperation and death, as it did for William Struve in Argenta—a placer and quartz camp about 15 miles west-northwest of Dillon in Beaverhead County.

*J*UST BEFORE CHRISTMAS, a German named William Struve committed suicide under the following circumstances: He has frequently expressed a desire to rush into the arms of grim death, because life had become a burden. About six weeks ago, he remarked that he knew two boys who had a bottle of strychnine, and he intended to work for them in order that he might obtain the poison and destroy himself. No attention was paid to his strange language, which he continued to use.

He tried to sell his axe and blankets for two drinks of whiskey, on the fatal day, but no person was mean enough to take undue advantage of his appetite. He said that he was going to die, and he told one of the boys that he would leave the axe and blankets to him. After returning to his cabin, perfectly sober, he procured some strychnine from a neighbor for the purpose of killing a bear which had a den in the vicinity. He then made some coffee, which he shared with a friend who happened to call upon him. When this gentleman returned to the cabin, in the course of an hour, Struve was dead.

The unfortunate man was a native of Hanover, Germany, and he was a relative of the celebrated statesman of that country who bears the same name. He was one of the pioneers of California, having emigrated to that state in 1848, and he possessed at one time a fortune which soon disappeared. During the last fall he came to Argenta City, and he was employed by the St. Louis and Montana Mining Company. Struve was an industrious and a good-natured citizen. His acquaintances deeply lament the state of mental depression which led him to deliberately terminate his existence, particularly in this season.

Virginia City Montana Post, December 29, 1866

Christmas in Virginia City, 1867

Montanans long have measured their particular culture by comparison with more sophisticated societies in other parts of the nation. Shortly after Christmas 1867, an anonymous correspondent for the *New York Tribune* described the holiday in a Montana placer mining camp—only four years after the initial strike at Alder Gulch.

*H*OLIDAYS IN THE Rocky Mountains are the most festive of all our festive occasions. Dull care is thrown far in the background, and business is subordinated to social and general enjoyment.

Christmas Day in Virginia City was one of the balmiest days I ever witnessed in any clime. I sat most of the day in an office with the windows and doors open, and a fire would have been uncomfortable. The air was as soft as an eastern spring, and the sun shone out upon the hills and cliffs with such warmth as to start their winter crowns of snow in murmuring streamlets down their rugged sides.

The city was gay throughout. The mines had poured forth their sturdy men to have a holiday frolic, and The Pony (the chief saloon) had crowded tables from early morning until the wee small hours.

The street auctions were unusually lively. The stores were swarming with customers of all classes, from the unshorn and unshaven mountaineer to the fashionable belle. The "sports" had their lively games, and billiards attracted nearly all the dignitaries of state to try their skill.

Sumptuous dinners were spread in various uninviting-looking shanties. Yet women's fair hands and fascinating faces made guests forget the rude architecture that encircled them. In the evening, my host Chapin gave a ball, and one hundred jolly people responded. Tickets were $20 each, but the supply was unequal to the demand.

A second floor over one of the large storerooms was fitted up most tastefully for the occasion. Evergreens and flowers were festooned around the walls, and the Stars and Stripes were hung in graceful folds over the orchestra.

For the first time in the far west, I found nearly as many ladies as men at the ball—although they were more varied in their ages than is usual in eastern gatherings of this kind. Young misses of 10 and 12 years were frequent partners. In my only active participation in the ball (the promenade to supper), my partner was a grandmother who owned up to nearly 60 winters.

Supper came at midnight, and it would have done credit to any eastern town of thrice our population. Oyster soup opened the course—the oysters having been shipped three thousand miles. Elegant salads, delicious jellies, game of all kinds, candies manufactured into temples and monuments, and almost every variety of fruits, plus sparkling wines, combined to tempt the appetite.

While there was freedom from the severe exactations of social rules in the east, there was the most scrupulous care on the part of all to restrain social freedom within the bounds of propriety. After an hour at the table, the middle-aged portion of the party returned to the ballroom, while the old folks and the little ones retired to their homes.

Altogether it was one of the most agreeable gatherings I have ever witnessed. And it was enjoyed by most of the company as only western people can enjoy social parties. With all the freedom of western life, I have never seen a man intoxicated at a ball or other social meeting. And the sincere cordiality evinced by the ladies toward each other would be an improvement on the more cultivated customs of the east.

New York Tribune, January 4, 1868, as quoted in
Montana Newspaper Association Insert series,
December 10, 1922

Christmas Reverie in Bozeman, 1867

To secure information from outlying settlements, many Montana newspapers during the territorial period used local correspondents. In this case a Virginia City newspaper relies for an account of Christmas activities in Bozeman upon the Reverend Davis Willson, a regular contributor to the *Montana Post*.

Reverend Willson arrived in Montana in 1866 and settled in Bozeman to serve as the community's first schoolteacher. He later operated a mercantile business in town. Reverend Willson became a full-time Presbyterian minister in the late 1870s, and he served the Gallatin Valley until his death, shortly before World War I.

A "Merry Christmas" and a "Happy New Year" to you and to all Montana. To the miner, the packer, the hunter, the merchant, the mechanic, and all! Aye! What a world of thought and a feeling of hopes and joys rest in those few little words! How often they have been repeated by dear and distant friends, and how, even now, through the "dark, backward, and abysm of time" their echo falls upon the enchanted ear like the rarest and the richest of music.

I sit by a blazing fireplace and listen to its murmuring song of comfort, and I see images in the fiery coals that add a sort of melancholy to the time. I look out from my window and the snow is falling—falling fast. From the misty atmosphere comes the memories of the New Year and the Christmas of times past, and what a change! But these little words are still whispering their sweet illusions, and neither time, nor circumstance, nor a suffering soul within could banish them from our hearts. A low howl comes from out of the mountains, and the dark storm clouds are hovering lower! God pity the help-less and the unclad. May we not forget, in our rejoicing, when we repeat the old-time greetings, there is another meaning in them that is half in prayer and half in doubt, when uttered for the poor and the unfortunate.

But with these sober remarks by way of introduction—and in the effort of keeping my communication balanced, should I carry our rejoicings too far—let me here make it known to all the world (for, no doubt, all the world is interested) that we of Bozeman have not been behind them in observing the holidays.

On the eventful Christmas Eve, all the Masons and all those who love the Masons met at the large and spacious Hall, 26 by 60, newly built in this place, for the purpose of having a grand entertainment in the way of dancing. Our company was honored by many friends from the West Gallatin, by our excellent Captain's lady from Fort Ellis, and by the fort's many gentlemanly

Riding the Range—Winter (detail), by Frederick Remington. From Frederick Remington, *Drawings* (New York, 1897), n.p.

officers—besides many of our fair and brilliant faces who inhabit the homely dwellings of stirring, enterprising Bozeman.

Who in the East shall henceforth say there is no society, no civilization here? To us, no rooms were ever decorated more gorgeously. Chandeliers never shone more brilliantly; hearts never beat more joyfully; music never thrilled more sweetly; refreshments never refreshed more refreshingly; social spirits never associated more socially; the "many twinkling feet" never twinkled to proportionate time or to dulcet airs more airily. Our friend Frazier is about to repeat the entertainment on New Year's Eve, when we are expected to glide from the old year to the new in the right time.

Virginia City Montana Post, January 4, 1868

An Affray in McClellan Gulch, 1867

In the rough-and-tumble society of Montana Territory's early placer mining camps, the Christmas holiday often prompted a serious drinking spree. And this activity easily could produce violence. Such was the case in 1867 at McClellan Gulch, located west of Stemple Pass and about 15 miles southeast of Lincoln.

A ROW OCCURRED in Dailey's Saloon in McClellan Gulch on Christmas Eve. In it one man was mortally wounded, and two other persons were severely wounded. It appears that a free and easy dance was in progress and, during the excitement, a "fast" Spanish woman named Rosella (formerly a resident of Helena, who was compelled to leave there for attempting the life of another woman) became involved in a quarrel with one of the men. Then Fanny Clark stepped in and offered to stand by her friend, Rosella.

At this point, John Smoot interfered on the part of the man, and a general fight resulted. During the melee, Smoot received a fearful cut in the abdomen by a knife. It is not known as yet by whom the knife was used. Rosella also received a severe blow over the head with a revolver, and a man named Doyle was badly cut. Medical assistance was sent for, but the messenger was drunk and became lost in the mountains. Smoot died on Thursday morning, before any assistance arrived. He was a young man, and we understand that his relatives reside in Blackfoot City.

Virginia City Montana Post, January 4, 1868

A Christmas with Bacchus in Helena, 1867

A large majority of Montana's mining-camp population consisted of young, single, hard-working men who were bent on striking it rich and getting out quickly. For many of these men, Christmas offered an excuse to drink heavily, to carouse, and generally to raise hell. Every camp included establishments that encouraged this form of holiday celebration, and some of these incidents became violent.

THE CELEBRATION of Christmas commenced here on Christmas Eve. As early as seven o'clock, we saw devotees of Bacchus reclining in positions more compact than graceful, on several of the steps that obstruct our sidewalks.

The liquor, billiard, gambling, and concert saloons and hurdy-gurdy houses were filled, and they remained so for two days. At some point, nearly every saloon had its own peculiar row. Any looker-on, bearing in mind the danger from stray shots, would make up his mind (as did the son of the quarreling family) that they "had a little hell of their own, and devils enough to tend it."

Main Street was the broad aisle through which the devotees of pleasure marched to do their idol homage. As they did so, their barbaric yells resounded throughout the town. They yelled just for the sake of yelling, as some babies do.

On Christmas night the orgies reached their height, but we can give no detailed description of them, for most of the participants had become so drunk as to cease to be amusing. The hurdy-gurdy house on the corner of West Main and Bridge Streets was so crowded that the heads were as close together as paving stones. At last commotion was here created among the carousers by the firing of fire-crackers surreptitiously tossed under their feet.

At the "Masquerade Ball" at Social Hall, tights, short dresses, and Spanish accents predominated. A large crowd was in attendance and forced the issue—witness the sixteen panes of glass missing the next morning from the Hall's front door.

At the Police Court there was disappointment. The harvest seemed ripe for the reaping, but it was not brought in. Thus the Justices had to pass a gloomy Christmas with only one poor little victim to console them.

At the *Herald* office, last but not least, the day was observed with that strict propriety which should characterize such a significant anniversary—and for which all those connected with newspaperdom, and especially with the *Herald* office, are justly noted.

Helena Weekly Herald, January 2, 1868

The Holidays in Deer Lodge, 1869

Because of its agricultural background, the town of Deer Lodge escaped some of the wild celebrations typical of Montana mining camps during the 1860s.

*L*IKE GOOD CHRISTIANS, as they are, Deer Lodgers have duly observed and enjoyed the gala week of the year. Care has been laid on the top shelf for seven days, and the undivided attention of the community has been given to looking at life through a rose-colored medium. Christmas Eve, Christmas Day, New Year's Eve, and the intervening time has been devoted to balls, calls, dinners, and social entertainments, with egg-nogg, skates, wheels, runners, etc., sandwiched in—and an occasional flirtation on the side, well done or rare, to suit the various ages and dispositions of the participants.

Deer Lodge only yields the palm to Virginia City as a social city, in a numerical point of view. In no community we have seen is hospitality more generously or courteously extended, or more pleasantly manifested is belief in the Whittier axiom that "in giving, there is gaining."

In the mountains here, the distinguishing characteristics of Christmas and New Year's, as observed in the East, have not yet been segregated and resolved, each unto its own. So, we had New Year's calls on Christmas, and we will probably have a little Christmas mixed up with New Year's. But even strawberries and cream are good served together.

So, if we like to do it that way, we'll do it. Very many of our ladies entertained their friends on Christmas, and we believe all will be pleased to exchange the compliments of the day with them on this New Year's Day.

Deer Lodge New North-West, December 31, 1869

Christmas with the Military in Prickly Pear Canyon, 1869

From its inception, Montana Territory featured a strong military presence. When they were garrisoned at military posts, these troops could celebrate Christmas in somewhat traditional ways. Yet, circumstances did not always afford such luxury—as James W. Ponsford recounts.

Ponsford was a 22-year-old officer at the time he was detailed from Fort Ellis (near present-day Bozeman) to Fort Shaw (west of Great Falls) and spent Christmas Eve in Prickly Pear Canyon, about 35 miles north of Helena. He subsequently received an honorable discharge and located in Bozeman, where he ran a series of saloons. In 1895 Ponsford also served in the patronage position of sergeant-at-arms in the Senate of the Montana Legislature. He died in Bozeman in 1912.

MAJOR EUGENE M. BAKER's troops hit Heavy Runner's camp on the morning of January 23, 1870. In the ensuing massacre, 173 Natives, including 53 women and children, lost their lives.

Campaigning against Indians when the weather is forty degrees below zero is no soft snap! And that was certainly the most disagreeable Christmas I have ever spent. It was the winter of 1869–1870, and there were more than two hundred troopers of the Second U.S. Cavalry camped in Prickly Pear Canyon on Christmas Eve. We were on our way from Fort Ellis to Fort Shaw, and then further to the Marias, where we were expected to attack the Blackfeet.

We were traveling light, for the march was a long one. Although the weather was cold, we didn't have many blankets.

And that winter of 1869–1870 was a cold one. I remember that we had reached Last Chance Gulch [Helena] without very much trouble, however. In fact, the first one hundred miles of the trip was made with less discomfort than any other part of it. But it was cold when we left Fort Ellis, and it got colder as we moved along.

Troops G, H, F, and L, stationed at Fort Ellis, had been ordered to join General [Regis] deTrobriand, in command of Fort Shaw, and from there to proceed into Indian country. You see, the Piegans and Blackfeet had been giving the whites no end of trouble that fall and winter. They had killed some freighters below Fort Benton and stolen a lot of horses. Besides, they had killed what few cattle they ran into, and they were threatening to the settlers in that part of the territory.

The Indians had killed several men before the department finally took up their case. I guess that the report went in pretty strong, for when the order came back from General [Philip H.] Sheridan, in command of the department, it left the commanding officers out here in no doubt as to what remained to be done. General Sheridan ordered them to "Strike the Indians, and strike them hard!"

Colonel [Eugene M.] Baker was in command of Fort Ellis then, and he led the expedition. We left the post near Bozeman one cold morning and struck out for Last Chance Gulch. We arrived there without any mishap and without serious inconvenience—except that it was cold.

Then it turned colder. I remember that we made camp in Prickly Pear Canyon on Christmas Eve. The thermometer showed it to be forty degrees below zero. We had some shelter tents along, but they were not much protection, and the men shivered around the big fires the early part of the evening.

The tents did help a little, however, and they went up as soon as we had come to a stop. We pitched the little A-shaped fellows right on the ice. We couldn't drive the tent pins in, and the way we managed that problem was a bit unusual. The men cut little holes in the ice at the corners of the tent, inserted the pins, and then poured water in the holes. In a few minutes, those pins were as firmly embedded in the ice as if they had been driven in the ground on a summer's day. That shows you how cold it was there in the canyon.

Prickly Pear Canyon, King and Gillete Toll Road-No. 2, by Peter Toftt (watercolor on paper, 1866). Montana Historical Society Museum, Helena

The men who had to stand guard that night suffered some, I can tell you. The rest of us fellows didn't fare much better. We had to keep moving some to keep our feet from freezing. I got pretty chilly along in the early hours of Christmas morning, but we soldiers hadn't any right to complain. And if we did kick, it didn't do us any good. On Christmas morning we made a lot of black coffee by our campfires and, after we had swallowed that, we commenced to feel better.

I don't remember what we had to eat on Christmas Day, but I do recall what we didn't have to drink. Our colonel had been very careful to see that no spirits were taken along on the trip, and that proved to be a mighty good thing. If the troopers had been allowed to drink what whiskey they had wanted, many of them would have been frozen to death that night. Whiskey is all right in its place, but its place is not on a long march when the mercury is trying to crowd out the bottom of a thermometer.

We reached Fort Shaw eight days after we left Fort Ellis. After resting up for a few hours, we struck out into the Indian country. We were reinforced with two companies of mounted infantry that had been stationed at Fort Shaw. Colonel Baker was in command of the troops. Our progress after we left Fort Shaw was rapid . . . The third morning out, we struck the camp of Heavy Runner on the Marias.

Helena Montana Daily Record, December 19, 1903

Mills Editorial, Deer Lodge, 1870

James H. Mills came to Montana in 1866 and soon assumed the editorship of the *Virginia City Montana Post,* the territory's first newspaper. In 1869 he founded the weekly *New North-West* in Deer Lodge, which he published for 22 years. Newspapermen widely considered Mills the preeminent editor of his time; they elected him the first president of the Montana Press Association. Mills died in 1904 and, in 1961, was inducted in the University of Montana School of Journalism's Hall of Fame. Mills's prose is consistently incisive, daring, resonant, and flowery in the Victorian style.

FOR SOME 1,500 YEARS, Christmas has pretty generally come once a year on the 25th of December. Nearly every newspaper in American—since that canny old Scotchman, John Campbell, set the example in the Boston News Letter in 1705—has annually devoted a column or so to a recital of the customs, causes, history, and hospitalities of the day. Therefore, there is not much new to be said on the subject, and such of the old as is forgotten is scarce worth repeating.

Christmas requires no exhortations to its observance or enjoyment. Although Dickens' Old Scrooge—who wished that "every idiot who goes about with 'Merry Christmas' on his lips might be boiled in his own pudding and buried with a stake of holly through his heart"—has, here and there, a pitiful counterpart in life, still the bells will ring the Christ-birth chimes right cheerily. And, from round-eyed prattlers to trembling age, the great world is happier and holier that its millions of hearts throb faster in the jovial Christmas-times.

It has been written, "Christmas comes but once a year; and when it comes, it brings good cheer." May it bring such to you—with never a care or heart-ache—that to all may come, in its fullness of grace, our best wishes for a Merry Christmas.

Deer Lodge New North-West, December 23, 1870

The Rev. Mr. Rommel and the Christmas Bazaar, 1872

After receiving a degree from Princeton University and Seminary, the Reverend Mr. William C. Rommel served as pastor of the First Presbyterian Church of Helena from 1872 to 1876. Following his term as a missionary in Montana, Rommel returned to New York State, where he engaged in several successful business ventures.

The Presbyterian bazaar, held in 1872 at the Masonic Temple, became an annual affair that helped to finance the first brick Presbyterian church in Helena. Each bazaar featured tables of handmade fancy goods for sale, lemonade and ice-cream tables, supper tables offering oyster stew and both chicken and turkey dinners, and a Christmas Day sit-down dinner "in the New England style." Alcohol was not served on the premises.

THE ROMAN CATHOLICS had raised a large sum of money the previous year by holding a Christmas bazaar, and our ladies decided to have a similar bazaar [to raise money for a church building]. They came to me full of the idea and enthusiasm. I approved cordially, but they innocently added, "And we will have dancing and raffling, and we will make lots of money for our church."

"What!" I said. "Have a dance and raffling for a Presbyterian Church?"

"Why, certainly," they replied. "The Roman Catholics made most of their money that way last winter."

I promptly said, "That cannot be." They insisted, and at last I said, "I have a valise; it is readily packed. I will not remain in charge of a Helena church if such a bazaar is undertaken."

"Oh, if you feel that way, we will not have the bazaar. But that is the only way to make any money here in Helena."

"Very well," I concluded. "I am satisfied."

Later they came penitently and said, "You were right, and we were wrong. We will have the bazaar without any of the objectionable features, but we will make very little money, perhaps $200. And the Roman Catholics are reported to have cleared $7,000 in three weeks."

We worked with a will and had the bazaar for three days, including Christmas Day. The gentlemen aided royally. Some washed and wiped dishes. At the Christmas dinner, Judge [Decius S.] Wade and others were the waiters and, at the end, over $800 was netted, and all were happy. The "boys" were astonished that they could leave the fair with any gold dust in their pockets, and they voted the Presbyterian bazaar all right.

The following Sunday night in the Odd Fellows' Hall (where we were meeting temporarily), I faced a full house of men, many of whom had aided us generously at the bazaar. I knew that Christmas had been a day of dissipation for many of them. I knew that the coming New Year's Day would be even more so—as the custom of our leading families was to keep open-house on that day and to offer refreshments, including liquor, to their guests. With a purpose, my text that night was "Look Not Upon the Wine When It Is Red."

I was young, ardent, and a convinced teetotaler. From the beginning to the end of the sermon, some of the men in the audience never raised their eyes from the floor. My peroration was an earnest appeal to the women of Helena not to offer intoxicants to their guests on New Year's Day.

The next morning, as I walked up Main Street, I was conscious of an atmosphere. Some men would not speak to me; some acted as if their necks had been stiffened. On entering the store of one of my congregation, he shook a warning finger and bade me to look out for myself. I asked why.

He replied, "Because of your temperance sermon last night!" I had suddenly become famous, or rather infamous. The idea of preaching a temperance sermon in Helena—and such a temperance sermon! I had quoted a remark of a friend, "All Helena's drunk on Christmas Day," in the sermon. This was taken up on the street with a vengeance. For example:

"Hello, Tom! I heard that you were drunk on Christmas."

"That's a damned lie! Who told you that?"

"Why, the Presbyterian preacher."

"When did he say that?"

"Last Sunday in his sermon." And then the poor preacher would get another cursing.

So the boys kept it up. One man told me years later that he was present at the sermon and had been under the influence of liquor on Christmas. But

Indian Camp in Winter—Crow Indians. Calfee and Catlin, photographers, Montana Historical Society Photograph Archives, Helena

he also had helped our bazaar liberally. He said that he was so angry that he had made up his mind to thrash me—but then he had changed his mind.

I was discouraged, feeling that I had only roused opposition. But on New Year's Day I made sixty calls, and in only two places was liquor served. In one of these cases (the International Hotel), the wife of the proprietor said to me, "I heard your sermon, and I agree with you. But my husband said that we must have liquor today. So I told him, 'Well, I will not serve it. We ladies will have our own table. If the gentlemen insist on having liquors, they may go over to that table and help themselves'."

Thus loyally did the ladies of Helena, Montana, on New Year's Day, 1873, respond to an appeal on behalf of their husbands, brothers, and sons.

Rev. George Edwards, "Presbyterian
Church History in Montana," *Contributions to the
Historical Society of Montana*, vol. 6 (Helena, 1907)

Christmas at Crow Agency, 1874

Dexter E. Clapp became Indian Agent at the Crow Agency in 1874 when it was located on Mission Creek, near Livingston. He moved the agency to the Stillwater Valley the following year. With the Reverend Matthew Bird and their wives, Agent Dexter directed a Christmas celebration that would both "Christianize and civilize" his young charges.

ON CHRISTMAS EVE we were favored with an entertainment at this Agency that certainly deserves more than a mere passing notice. The entertainment referred to was given by the Mission School, under the charge of our worthy pastor, Reverend Mr. Bird, which so far exceeded anything in the reasonable range of expectation that I cannot forbear giving it all of my attention.

When I witnessed the performance of these children (who, but one year ago, were living the nomadic life common to our Western tribes), united in diversified melodies, declamations, the Lord's Prayer, and various other exercises—in a manner surprisingly faultless—I was overwhelmed with astonishment and filled with admiration. I could but regret that the citizens of

Bozeman were not present to note the wonderful progress made by these native children, through the persistent efforts of your former fellow-citizen, the Reverend Mr. Bird.

The exercises of the evening were closed by the distribution of presents from the traditional Christmas tree, which were ample, and of a character suitable to the wants and tastes of the recipients.

This latter part of the programme, being under the exclusive supervision of the estimable wife of the newly appointed Agent, Mrs. D. E. Clapp, was in every respect a very decided success. Her mind, every ready to invent some means of enjoyment and comfort for these little wards, first conceived the idea of a Christmas tree on this occasion. To her ingenious hands—assisted by Mrs. Bird, Miss Noteware, and Mrs. McMillan—are we mainly indebted for the beautiful evergreen wreaths, festoons, emblems, etc., which served so admirably in decorating the Church. And to her are we also indebted for a select poem, in its rendition far surpassing anything we have had the pleasure of hearing in the West, and could not have failed to elicit commendation in circles much farther east than Crow Agency.

The Church was filled to its utmost capacity. There were present the pale face, the red face, and those who had claim to both. And there was no mistaking the fact that the entire medley enjoyed to the fullest extent the finest, the rarest, the most interesting, and by far the most satisfactory entertainment ever given at Crow Agency.

Bozeman Avant Courier, January 1, 1875

Eggs the Coin of the Realm, 1874

The traditional Christmas drink on the Montana frontier was egg nog, when it could be obtained. Little difficulty was encountered in providing the whiskey and rum for the concoction; it was the eggs that were scarce.

ABOUT CHRISTMAS TIME, this fruit looms up in price. One dozen eggs will get three pounds of coffee or four pounds of sugar at Strasburger and Sperling's. Twelve yards of the best calico only costs eighteen eggs. One egg will buy a glass of lager at Manej's; six will get a square meal at Dutch John's; two dozen eggs will get one of those nice glass jars of honey at Rich and Willson's.

And the barter continues: five pounds of hominy will be given for one dozen eggs at A. Lamme and Company's; a fancy shawl at Ellis and Davis' for two dozen eggs; six dozen will buy a sack of XXX flour at McAdow and Brother's Gallatin mills; Sheriff Clark will serve a writ for a dozen fresh eggs; Brother Iliff will marry a nice couple for two dozen; and the *Avant Courier* for one full year can be had for five dozen eggs. It is astonishing what can be done with eggs just now.

Bozeman Avant Courier, December 18, 1874

Christmas in Bozeman, 1874

Slowly the celebration of Christmas in Montana Territory assumed the more staid characteristics of a holiday in the Midwest or the East.

*O*NE NEED NOT be very aged to remember his Presbyterian grand-father's holy horror when the Episcopal church bells rang out Christmas, nor the time when Christmas trees were nothing less than Popish abominations. A Gothic window, or a cross upon a steeple was enough to turn any deacon's stomach in those days—and all the women in the congregation had the cramps at the mention of a Christmas tree. But those times have passed away, and Christmas has become a thing of joy to all in the land.

In accordance with local custom, the Sunday School had its tree on Christmas Eve and, long before the hour, the Church was filled to overflowing. The tree was a very fine one and was loaded down with gifts. After a musical service by the school, the gifts were distributed, under the paternal supervision of Mr. Horr as Santa Claus—who was the exact counterpart of the old man we once imagined popped down the chimneys of our youth.

Every thing passed off pleasantly, and great praise is due the ladies who had the arrangements in charge and who exerted themselves to the utmost to give success to the undertaking.

The last Legislature prohibited the firing of guns or pistols within the town limits, or near any public gatherings. We commend the law to the attention of those who have been celebrating Christmas in Bozeman by the banging of firearms.

Bozeman Times, December 29, 1874

A Philipsburg Christmas

Those mining camps that proved successful and developed semi-permanent populations quickly became focuses for more formal holiday festivities. The occasion of a Christmas Day wedding elicited special comment.

*T*HE O'CONNOR BALL on Christmas Eve was a success in the full sense of the word. It was well-attended—the ladies never looked more beautiful, nor the gentlemen more gallant. Imagine the effect on an old "bach" who has the weakness to estimate the ladies just a little higher than the angels. If they were the gods to be worshipped, the happiness of eternity would be secured to some of us.

The little folks were not forgotten, and were made glad with full stockings on Christmas morning.

In the Old Days the Cow Ranch Wasn't Much, by Charles M. Russell (pen and ink, 1925). Montana Historical Society Museum, Helena

The great event of all was the wedding, on Christmas Day, of Peter Jessen, of the Upper Deer Lodge Valley, to Miss Alice M. Jansen, the daughter of Neil Jansen, of this place—with G. C. Vineyard, Justice of the Peace, officiating. Here is a Christmas present that throws all others in the shade; one that will bring to the parties a lifetime of joy, contentment, and happiness, which will increase each year of their lives as other little Christmas presents accumulate. Miss Jensen, in the time she has resided in this place, has endeared herself to many, whose best wishes go with her in her new relation.

Deer Lodge New North-West, January 7, 1876

The Butte Christmas Gathering, 1876

In the mid-1870s, Butte's population ranged between 1,200 and 1,500 people. The mining camp perched on the eve of the explosive development of its underground copper lodes. However, when town leaders attempted to produce a community-wide Christmas event (rather than the separate Christmas-tree celebrations usually held in each church), difficulties developed among factions of the population. After 1876, it would be decades before Butte tried another community-wide celebration at Christmas.

*O*N CHRISTMAS NIGHT, old and young turned out to see the tree that, for a week at least, had been in preparation. Mesdames John Noyes, H. Young, and Preston Scott, the committee appointed to select the presents and to decorate the tree, were so anxious to make the gathering for the children as pleasant as possible that they had spared no expense, time, or labor. And we are glad to be able to say that their efforts were fully rewarded, for the tree was really very handsomely dressed and the presents selected were, in every respect, suitable for the children.

Some croakers were heard to say that, although the tree itself was handsome, the base was left unfinished; they suggested that moss and artificial flowers would have added greatly to the effect. Though some such thought had occurred to us, we realized fully the exertion that had been required to accomplish what had already been done and felt that thanks instead of fault-finding was due the ladies for all of their trouble.

Some considerable feeling has been manifested since the event, and from what we know of the facts, there is cause for complaint. It seems that many presents known to have been put upon the tree failed to go into the hands of those for whom they were intended. In fact, they disappeared—nobody knows exactly when or how. It is quite certain, nevertheless, that several articles were actually taken from the tree at some period between the time of its completion and the distribution.

When all were assembled and all seated that could be accommodated, Mr. William Porter, in the guise of Saint Nicholas, appeared in the midst of the company and, taking his stand in front of the brilliantly lighted tree, began to distribute the presents. Some of those girls—or young ladies (begging their pardon)—who had reached the age of fourteen must have wished "I were a child again," as the presents furnished by the committee were given only to those who came between the ages of 2 and 13. The value of the gifts, knowing as we do the price that such goods necessarily command here, astonished us! That was the best evidence of the success of the entertainments previously given to raise the Christmas Tree Fund.

Some persons took occasion to pay off old scores by sending gifts to be distributed from the tree. And some of these articles savored decidedly of the practical, so much so as to be, in one or two instances, somewhat indelicate. The original programme was to have had the friends of the children, after the distribution of the presents, partake of a dance, but some unpleasantness occurred among those assembled, which terminated matters rather abruptly. This is to be regretted, as it became evident then and there that there is no longer any comfort to be derived from an informal public gathering in Butte. In other words—from a mixed crowd.

Notwithstanding these grievances above mentioned, the main object of the event was accomplished and the children made happy. We, among others present, made joyous from seeing the little folks so well pleased—so much so that, when next Saint Nick comes, "May we be there to see."

Butte Miner, January 2, 1877

Mills Christmas Editorial, 1876

George H. Mills, founder of the _Deer Lodge New North-West,_ was recognized throughout Montana as the territory's premier editor. In typical Victorian prose, Mills penned an annual Christmas editorial for his readers—a tradition in which he delighted.

$\mathscr{C}$HRISTMAS IS the brightest day in all the calendar for the little folks. Blessed be the Christmas Holiday, with its holly, mistletoe, and snow; its brilliant gift-laden trees; its memories of a Savior's love and sacrifice; its interchange of heart-tendered mementoes; its laughing lips and brightened eyes; its music, praise, and song; its glowing fires and laden boards; its revelry, mirth, and devotions.

Without it, Winter would be drear indeed; without the Love it commemorates, life would be hopeless and memory a curse; without it, childhood would be a monotonous round of soiled clothes and scant playhouses and age but a perilous groping on the deceitful shores of a fathomless sea. No Christmas, and the White Cross of Faith would be a meaningless symbol; no Christmas, and laughter would be gone out of the world; no Christmas, and mothers' hearts would beat less happily as they clasped their babes, while children would gaze vacantly on collapsed stockings and the triumphant turkey strut out a useless existence amid the unconscious cows.

No! Take away our other blessings, but leave us Christmas time! Take from us gently but firmly the lower story of our January thermometer; remove into the Barken desert or some other uninhabited place the tax collector and the newspaper canvasser; but leave us the Christmas tree and a moderate allowance of egg-nogg. Let coarsest covering fend our feet from frost, but give us daintiest hose for the little ones to hang on Christmas Eve. Let Tell and Mars be proven myths, but save to us the biographic truths of Crusoe and a merry, unfaltering faith in glorious old Santa Claus.

Then will men and matrons and the eager-eyed elfs be joyous, if but for one day in the great round year. And while the lowering skies touch with gracious fingers the brown earth to clothe it in the immaculate and to give us a white Christmas, may the grace of the All Father fill our hearts with Charity, Love, and Good Will—till their whiteness shall rival the snow.

Deer Lodge New North-West, December 22, 1876

C. W. Savage's Christmas in Miles City, 1876

The recognition that Montana Christmas celebrations were shaped by the rawness and uncertainty of the frontier is nowhere better illustrated than in this story told by Charles W. Savage about his experiences at Fort Keogh in 1876. It should be remembered that he is recounting the first Christmas following the Battle of the Little Big Horn, fought in June of that year.

Savage remained in southeastern Montana, and ran a mercantile business in Miles City into the 1880s. He was one of the prime organizers of Custer County (1877), was elected its first County Treasurer, was appointed the first postmaster of Miles City, and was elected sheriff of Custer County. At the time of his death in 1903, he was operating the Leighton Hotel in Miles City.

I SPENT MY first Christmas in Montana right here, near Miles City. That was the winter of 1876, and I had just come from Minnesota with a stock of goods for the Keogh cantonment. There were here then about ten companies of the Fifth U.S. Infantry under Colonel Nelson Miles, and at that time there wasn't any real town here.

When the post tradership was decided, all of us other men with stocks of goods had to leave. So we laid out a town about two miles below here, on the Yellowstone River. Then, in 1878, when the present town was laid out, we all moved back up here.

That Christmas of 1876 was a very pleasant one. I don't remember that we have ever since had better Christmas weather than it was then. The soldiers were at the cantonment, and they had a big time on Christmas.

There were plenty of Indians around here in those days. No one thought of going anywhere unless he was well-armed—and even then he took chances. On that Christmas I remember seeing a number of Sioux Indians killed on the flats right close to town here.

A lot of Sioux had approached the cantonment and had shown a flag of truce. They wanted to talk with the commanding officer, and preparations were being made to receive them. Then, suddenly, the Crow Indians with the troops charged out and attacked them. They killed half a dozen of the Sioux. It seems that they paid no attention at all to the flag of truce.

Well, the attackers knew what the Colonel would do to them. So, after they had killed all of their old-time enemies that they could, they swam the Yellowstone and cleared out. There was ice floating in the river, but they didn't stop on that account. Going up the river, they crossed it again and made for their own country. A memorable Christmas that one was!

Helena Montana Daily Record, December 19, 1903

A Miner's Christmas in the Hills, 1870s

When William C. Vipond died in his cabin in Bear Gulch, near Twin Bridges, in 1921, he was recognized across Montana as one of the state's pioneer prospectors. After arriving in Montana Territory in 1864, Billie and his brother made several significant strikes, including ones up Quartz Canyon Creek, near Divide. As a result, the Vipond Mining District in this area south of Butte was named for him. Perhaps no prospector could better speak to the issue of spending Christmas in the mountains of Montana, since he enjoyed it decade after decade.

*H*ow DOES an old prospector spend Christmas? Why, that depends upon who he is and where Christmas overtakes him. If he happens to be in a country remote from civilization, holed up in the mountains where nothing save an occasional zephyr whistling through the branches of the majestic pines disturbs the placid serenity of his surroundings, it is doubtful if he knows when the day arrives.

He knows, however, that there is such a day as Christmas, and that it would be nice to celebrate it according to Hoyle, but he is too busy watching the changes in the formation of the rock of his claim to keep track of the days, and is therefore practically lost to the world. He may have a calendar in his little log cabin to assist him in remembering that there are seven days in each week, but even then he cannot determine which is which. All days look alike to him. Men segregated from populous communities in this western country have been known to lay aside their work on Wednesday, under the impression that the day is Sunday.

One old prospector who did this is William Vipond who, with his brothers, discovered the Vipond Mining District in Beaverhead County some years ago. With several other prospectors, he had gone into the mountains of a remote district early in the fall and had soon lost track of the days. Having been taught in youth that Sunday was a day of rest and worship, the party decided to observe the day, but when an attempt was made to determine which day was Sunday, it was found that the calendar with which the party had provided itself would not work.

For there were no church bells to aid in solving the problem; no closed stores or display of gaudy apparel to give the party a pointer. But here were socks and shirts to be washed once in a while. So it was argued that Sunday would be as good a day as any on which to do these chores.

The calendar was consulted many times. Finally one of the party counted up the days he thought he and his companions had been in the mountains, and Sunday was located. But when the party returned to civilization the following spring, it was discovered that the location was four days wrong on one side and three days on the other. Mr. Vipond is now in Butte and often refers to the time that he and his companions observed Wednesday for Sunday.

The prospector who knows when Christmas arrives nearly always makes some provision to celebrate the day. If in the mountains of the north, some other class of game graces his table. Whether north or south, if an old prospector can get hold of a flag, the star-spangled banner floats from the highest point on the cabin. And, if he cannot secure a real flag, an old red shirt takes its place. In the absence of both, there is no real Christmas for the mountain mineralogist.

In sections where there are several men located in different cabins, the whole crew, in everyday garb, usually gathers under the roof of the one that has the best layout, and there celebrates the day in a manner as commendable as the exigencies of the occasion will admit. Each one contributes to the feast and, unless the period of separation from civilization has been a long one, the Christmas dinner is not so bad. The boys just simply have a feast, play cards, if they have any, recall the days when, as youngsters, they waited for Santa, and discuss the possibilities of striking the pay-streak before Christmas comes again.

A prospector's Christmas is not a bad one. The man who has spent his life in the mountains is just as happy and content with his little fry of bacon and stew of applesauce, if he has nothing else, as the man who rolls in the lap of luxury in the city. If he has good things to eat, he will eat them and look pleasant and, if he has not been fortunate enough to acquire them, he will accept what he has and look just as pleasant. He is a philosopher and king of the woods. Believing that some day things will come his way, he makes the most of the situation without finding fault with either himself or someone else.

Some prospectors never pay much attention to Christmas or any other holiday. They are too busy hunting for that which they always feel sure they will find. Their work and the prospects for striking it rich are more fascinating to them than a thousand holidays merged into one. They do not even recognize Sunday, but for 365 days in the year toil away with visions of the pretty yellow metal as their goal. Indeed, the miner's Christmas in the mountains is not the city way.

Anaconda Standard, December 21, 1902

Statehood and Industrialization

*T*HE ARRIVAL of the transcontinental railroad to Montana in 1883 became its most significant nineteenth-century event. Trains changed transportation and settlement patterns, and they challenged the core attitudes of a rapidly growing population of non-Indians. For all practical purposes, the railroad forced the restriction of various tribes to specific reservations. It brought commercial ties to the rest of the nation, and it precipitated a strong statehood movement. Finally accomplished in 1889, statehood legitimized Montana to its citizens, giving hope to many who desired to establish a genteel respectability modeled after eastern social customs.

Montana's railroad network spurred the development of many of the new state's resources, from livestock to timber to copper. Suddenly Butte became Montana's first and only city, and the "War of the Copper Kings" played out in statewide arenas. As communities grew in size and diversity, Christmas events reflected community vigor and sophistication. Group charity assumed an important role; Montana was maturing.

Maiden, Montana Territory, 1885. W. H. Culver, photographer, Montana Historical Society Photograph Archives, Helena

Murder on Christmas in Billings, 1882

Despite the move towards gentility, holidays on the frontier frequently involved the extensive use of alcohol among its young men. As a result, violence often accompanied holiday celebrations, especially in regions where respectability and rawness were entwined. In the fledgling settlement of Billings in 1882, such was the case.

*J*EREMIAH COKELY was found guilty of second-degree murder in the Custer County District Court in April 1883, and sentenced to twelve years in the Territorial Prison.

Between the hours of 12 midnight and 1 a.m., on Christmas Eve, a sad encounter took place at the railroad section house. It resulted in the death of Patrick Dwyer, at the hands of one of his comrades, Jeremiah Cokely. Immediately after the tragedy, Cokely left the scene of death and walked down the street and stood talking with Matt Rademaker, at the rear of McAdow's Store. Then the officers, accompanied by a number of men, approached, surrounded, and shortly captured him with little resistance.

Dwyer was the foreman for this section of the Northern Pacific; he was a man who was generally liked by the men under his charge, although some said that he was a bully when he drank. He is said to have relatives in New York who were partially dependent upon him for support.

John Fitzgerald, Samuel Davis, and William Baker delivered evidence at the inquest, from which we extracted the following story of the circumstances which preceded and attended Dwyer's death:

Dwyer and a number of the section men were in Dwyer's room celebrating Christmas Eve by drinking beer. Cokely, meanwhile, was lying on Dwyer's bed, drunk and vomiting. There seems to have been a dispute over the beer question, and some persons in another room called Dwyer a liar. He was greatly incensed and, seizing a coal shovel, he rushed into the other room and threatened to kill Robert Crooks.

He then got his revolver, which had previously been consigned to Davis' care and, coming again into his own room, his attention was attracted by the fact that Cokely had vomited upon his bed. He made Cokely arise and marched him out of the room with the revolver at his head, and ordered him abed. Cokely then wanted a hat, and William Baker handed him Dwyer's hat—whereat Dwyer said that he would get Cokely's hat from the hall and left the room for that purpose.

Then Cokely produced his revolver and, with profane threat, announced his intention of shooting Dwyer. He then started to meet Dwyer and, as soon as he saw him, fired two shots. Dwyer cried out, "Oh! Jerry, I am shot!" and then took a step or two and fell, his revolver in his hand.

Dr. Sabin was summoned, but Dwyer was dead ere he reached him—one of the shots having taken effect in his breast and the other in his stomach. Both the prisoner and his victim seem to have been drinking hard, and the deceased was evidently in a very excited state of mind.

Early in the morning, Justice of the Peace J. D. Matheson, acting as coroner, made inquisition into the cause of death. The jury empaneled, after viewing the body and listening to the evidence of the parties above named, rendered the following verdict:

"That the said Patrick Dwyer came to his death from wounds caused by two bullets from a revolver in the hands of Jeremiah Cokely, on the 25th day of December, A.D. 1882, at the said town of Billings, in Custer County."

Untitled (pen and ink, circa 1899), by Charles M. Russell. Great Falls Elks Club Collection, Montana Historical Society Museum, Helena.

At 12 o'clock noon the prisoner was brought before Justice Matheson for preliminary examination. He waived examination and was committed to jail to await trial at the next session of court.

Billings Herald, December 28, 1882

Christmas in a Railroad Graders' Camp in Glendive, 1882

The Northern Pacific Railroad entered Montana Territory in 1881 and proceeded to construct sections of the mainline until the transcontinental was completed in 1883. Since most of this year-round work required hand labor and horses, large numbers of tough, young men were needed. The Christmas holiday in one of these construction camps found the men thousands of miles from their homes.

*C*HRISTMAS in a railroad graders' camp!

It may not sound pleasant to those who have never spent that holiday away from home and to whom the mere word brings up recollections of brilliantly lighted and heavily laden trees and of merry times when the entire family was gathered at the old homestead. But there are others in the world beside those who dwell in houses and who have a settled place that they call home.

A railroad graders' camp is one of the roughest places in the world. In this western country, when the great trunk lines were pushed through the valleys and over the mountains of a new state, the work attracted a particularly cosmopolitan crowd of men. There were the large groups of Irish, the Swedes, the Italians, the Chinese, and men of many other nationalities— often laborers picked up here and there throughout the West. In some camps these men were grouped by nationalities to reduce friction. Thus the Northern Pacific Railroad camp near Glendive, in 1882, was composed primarily of young Swedes.

Now in Sweden, Christmas is the greatest festal day of the year. Much is made of the holiday and, no matter in what part of the world he may be, the thoughts of a Swede return on Christmas Day to the land of his nativity.

In the winter of 1882–1883, the Northern Pacific had pushed beyond Glendive, then a tent town of almost 3,000 population. There are a few persons still in Dawson County who remember that Christmas. Among them is August A. Anderson, who for many years has been a passenger conductor on the Northern Pacific between Glendive (where he resides) and Billings. Mr. Anderson recalls:

"I remember that Christmas of 1882 very well. I don't know that I ever spent a more pleasant Christmas than that one. There was a big crowd of young Swedes in the grading camp, located two miles west of Glendive. And we decided to have a celebration on the same order that we would have had in the old country.

"Three of us lived in a cave that winter. There was Sam Samuelson and Andrew Andrewson and myself in the party. Early in the winter we had dug

The Northern Pacific Railroad rotary snowplow clears the way, winter 1887–1888. F. Jay Haynes, photographer, Haynes Foundation Collection, Montana Historical Society Photograph Archives, Helena

a cave in a high bank. We had first cut a doorway and then cut out a room about ten feet square. We had then dug out a fireplace and—with the aid of a large number of powder cans, which strewed the right-of-way—we built a chimney and had as comfortable a home as you could imagine.

"Now, Christmas Eve in Sweden is the greatest time of all the year, and we Swedes resolved to celebrate in the old-time style. Going to Glendive, we bought five gallons of cognac, and with that we brewed a punch that was simply nectar to the Swedes. The punch was served Christmas Eve in our little cave. The room was so small that the boys, after taking a drink or two, had to leave in order to give the fellows outside a chance. But, by coming in relays that way, the entire camp was served with punch.

"We had a very merry time of it that Christmas Eve. We sang the songs of the Old Country and told stories of other days when we had celebrated the festival in the Old Country. As I said, I have never spent a more pleasant Christmas.

"That old cave may still be seen in that high bank two miles west of Glendive. The roof fell in years ago, but the cave is still there. It is gradually being washed away, however, and I guess one more spring will serve to destroy it. There were three other caves in the bank. In one of them lived our foreman.

The Kimball girls, Missoula, circa 1914. Montana Historical Society Photograph Archives, Helena

He had a window in his cave, as befitting his station, but I don't think he was much more comfortable than we three. The other men lived in tents that winter, and that was pretty cold business, let me tell you.

"I don't recall what the weather was like on Christmas, but in the following February I know that it was 60 degrees below zero one morning. That was a morning too cold for Swedes, even, and I recall that we didn't work that day. All in all, though, I would not trade any winter for my winter in the graders' camp—and especially for our old-time Swedish Christmas."

Helena Montana Daily Record, December 19, 1903

Holiday Events in Lewistown, 1885

The settlement of Lewistown was in its infancy in 1885—by all accounts a rough, frontier village. On the Fourth of July the year before, "Rattlesnake Jake" Fallon and "Longhair" Owen had been killed in a shootout on Lewistown's main street. Still, the settlement carried some pretenses of civilization, and its residents determined to celebrate the Christmas holiday in style.

*W*E ARE HAVING a most pleasant winter here in the Judith Basin and a grand time enjoying ourselves with social parties and dances.

On Thursday evening, December 24th, a successful social dance was held at Maiden, and on December 25th a ball and supper was given by W. Hortop, the proprietor of the Hortop House in Lewistown. Mr. Hortop is a gentleman and, when he opens his house for a dance, everybody goes.

Mr. Hortop engaged the Maiden Brass and String Band, and the music was excellent; a better brass band was never organized. At Mr. Hortop's ball, the dancing was continued until 6 o'clock, a.m. The supper was a credit to the house, for a better one has not been served in this part of the country. Mrs. Doty superintended the supper in a manner to please everyone; she had the ballroom beautifully decorated.

Among the guests at the party were merchants, mechanics, stockmen, and cowboys—not the cowboys we read about in dime novels, but the gentlemanly cowboy of the Judith. They are a fine lot of boys, respected by all.

The ladies were dressed in elegant ball costumes, in the latest designs of fashion, and it is doubtful if even Helena can get up a finer party than this one at Mr. Hortop's.

Billings Montana Stock Gazette, December 31, 1885

The First Christmas Tree in Great Falls, 1885

Robert Vaughn was born in Wales in 1836, and he arrived in the United States in 1856 and in Montana Territory in 1864. He became one of the pioneer stockmen in the Sun River Valley; he assisted Paris Gibson mightily in the establishment of Great Falls in 1883. Until his death in 1918, "Uncle Bob" Vaughn proved one of the civic leaders of both Great Falls and Cascade County.

I WELL REMEMBER the first Christmas tree in Great Falls—which then was the village of Great Falls, for there were but a few houses here at the time. And most of them were small shacks, located on First and Second Avenues South.

A few days ago I was talking with Mrs. W. P. Beachly, who took an active part in that memorable gathering. It was in 1885 that this Christmas celebration took place, and it was held in the old frame schoolhouse, on the south side, which then had just been built. There were about thirty children in the district. W. P. Beachly, Phil Gibson, and Bert Huy furnished the tree and the evergreens for decorations.

Mrs. W. Pratt, Mrs. Will Hanks, and Mrs. W. P. Beachly did the decorating and arranged the tree. They also secured about $100 to purchase presents, most of which had to be brought from Helena. There were but two small stores in town then: Murphy, Maclay and Company, located in the old building across Central Avenue from the post office, of which W. P. Wren was the manager; Beachly Brothers and Hickory, who ran their store and kept the post office where Wocasek's Saloon is now, on Central Avenue.

It was a remarkably mild fall that year. The ferry on Broadwater Bay was running on the day before Christmas. The few settlers that were within the radius of ten miles were invited to attend, and all of them came. The schoolhouse was crowded to the steps, on the outside. For all that, everyone received a present.

W. P. Wren got a large doll, dressed in a pillow slip. Professor Mortson was presented with a pair of doll-baby twins, which he kissed and hugged dearly. A barrel of apples was gotten for the occasion and, before the closing, everybody was eating apples.

That night the first snow of the winter fell, and on Christmas Day the ground was covered with six inches of snow. By the last of December, the temperature had dropped to 20 below zero. Still, the winter was no way as severe as the next one [known as "The Hard Winter of 1886–1887"].

There are 25 or 30 people who are now residents of Great Falls who well remember the Christmas tree celebration referred to, among whom are: H. O. Chowen; Howard Criss; Joe Hamilton; George W. Dunlap; E. B. Largent; Charles Wegner; W. P. Wren; Phil and Theodore Gibson; Ira Meyers; Dr. [John H.] Fairfield; N. C. Dickinson; Ed Canary; W. P. Beachly; William Wamer; Dr. [Alfred G.] Ladd. In

Christmas in the Charles Suiter home, Butte, 1903. Montana Historical Society Photograph Archives, Helena

addition, there is our worthy United States Senator, Paris Gibson, who is the father of Great Falls.

Here, 17 years ago, there were but one small schoolhouse and one teacher. Now there are six elegant schoolhouses, occupied by 2,300 pupils, who are receiving their instruction from 53 teachers.

Great Falls Tribune, December 21, 1902

A Résumé of Christmas Activities in Billings, 1885

To many observers, the extent to which a frontier town was "civilized" was demonstrated by its celebration of major holidays. Only three years after Cokely's fatal shooting of Dwyer, the railroad town of Billings had settled down.

*C*HRISTMAS **D**AY dawned clear and glorious, with the mercury standing at 20 degrees above zero. After sunrise, the temperature rose rapidly until it reached the 50s, and some of our citizens were observed sporting their summer straw hats.

The first excitement in the morning was the explanation of the cabalistic legend "Watch 500," which has been puzzling many citizens for the past fortnight. All was made clear by the "Famous Outfitters," who distributed 500 loaves of bread, in many of which were hidden tickets entitling the possessor to prizes in money and goods. No charge was made, everyone carrying off as much bread as he chose, and the staff of life was soon scattered all over town.

Skating was taken up early in the day, it having been discovered that ice on the slough near Coulson was strong enough to bear. The hardware men sold large numbers of skates, and the purchasers had a good time all around.

The shooting match, for Pierce's poultry, attracted a number of crack shots. The finest work was done by Sam Wilde, who knocked the heads off three turkeys, with three successive shots, and generously bestowed the birds on parties who needed them more than he did. Louis Fenske and Jim Smith were also successful in hitting turkeys.

The firm of Robinson and Hannauer offered a fine seal-skin cap to the person who should make the nearest guess at the number of beans in a jar. The guesses were numerous and various, the highest being 34,343, and the lowest 900. The nearest guess was made by conductor James Conroy, who guessed 4,300. When the count was made, it was found that the jar contained 4,303 beans.

Hersey and Company awarded an elegant china tea set of 70 pieces, to be drawn for by their customers. Each purchaser of goods for the last two weeks to the value of one dollar was given a numbered ticket. On Christmas Eve, duplicate tickets were all put in a box and well shaken, and the first number drawn took the prize. Mr. C. A. Westum's ticket #46 carried off the crockery.

Church services were held in the morning at the Court House by the Reverend Alfred Brown, who preached a sermon appropriate to the occasion.

A highly successful entertainment was held at the Congregational Church last evening, under the auspices of the Sunday School of that Church. A general invitation had been extended to all the children in town to attend and to share in the festivities, the result being that the Church was filled.

Vocal and instrumental music, recitations, and pantomimes occupied the early part of the evening—and then occurred the big event—viz: The Christmas Ship, a full-rigged schooner, which sailed onto the stage laden with three 100-pound packages of candy, with unlimited quantities of oranges and apples for ballast. Judge Goss, A. S. Douglass, F. S. Bacon, and E. B.

Christmas card with drawing by E. W. "Bill" Gollings, 1930. Gift of Richard E. Crane, Montana Historical Society Museum, Helena

Camp distributed the good things. Every child received a full share and departed filled with satisfaction and candy. Much credit is due to the consignor who freighted the ship to a large and appreciative number of consignees.

The Dancing School gave a dance in McKee's Opera House, where about 40 couples enjoyed a good time. Professor Moore's orchestra made their first appearance at a dance, and they won high praise for their excellent music.

Private parties were numerous, and many families entertained their friends to dinner, where full and complete justice was done to the ample supply of turkey, plum pudding, and the other viands customary on such occasions.

Take it all in all, the day was a great success. Sobriety marked the conduct, and no arrests were made by the police. The amount of goods sold by our merchants for presents was immense. An especial run was made on toys, which no doubt gladdened the hearts of many little ones. To all, the day appeared to be a Merry Christmas.

Billings Montana Stock Gazette, December 31, 1885

A Superior Christmas, 1887

In the 1880s, the remote area around Superior supported trapping, mining and some lumbering, but had only limited winter access southeastward to Missoula via the Clark's Fork River. A correspondent from Superior let Missoulians know how their neighbors fared during the holidays.

*O*UR LETTER FROM SUPERIOR—Dear Mr. Editor: In your personal items a week or so ago, mention was made of old-timers from Superior being in Missoula, laying in supplies so they might be able to spend Christmas in a Christian-like manner. I intend that their friends in Missoula should know how they proceeded to carry out the ideas formed while smiling on the good things in Missoula.

In response to invitations, but few were absent from roll call on Christmas Day at Superior. The early settlers were pleased to join with late residenters, who added grace and beauty to the gathering. The first thing on the programme was shooting for turkeys, after which came dinner. The night was spent with songs and dancing till break of day. Then the company left for their several homes, promising to be at Mr. John Slowey's place for the New Year's Eve dance.

Missoula County Times, January 25, 1888

Christmas at the Fort Shaw Indian School, 1893

Fort Shaw (located on the Sun River, about 25 miles west of Great Falls) operated as a military post from 1867 to 1890. In 1892 the complex became the Fort Shaw Indian School, run by the United States Indian Service to educate students from several Montana tribes. Under the guidance of William H. Winslow, the school developed an industrial-arts curriculum with many supplemental programs. By Christmas of 1893, the facility almost had reached its capacity of 250 students and 35 teachers. The controversy continues concerning the validity of forced education and assimilation for Native American children.

*L*AST SATURDAY evening, the pupils of the Fort Shaw Indian School rendered the following program as a Christmas entertainment:

Music	Orchestra
Song	School
Recitation	Jennette Trexler
Christmas Star	Little Girls
Character Songs	Large Boys
Essay	Nancy Shepherd
Clarinet Solo	Paul Walters
Dialogue	"Santa Claus' Authority"
Song	Little Girls
Fancy Drill	Little Boys
Character Song	Large Boys
Recitation	Oliver Villeaux
Tableaux	"Christmas Eve"
Song	School
Music	Orchestra

We have received no report of the proceedings, but we venture the opinion that all of the little folks did very well.

Choteau Montanian, December 29, 1893

A Christmas Editorial in Hard Times, Helena, 1893

Robert E. Fisk's Christmas editorial in 1893 was particularly heartfelt. The Crash of 1893 had crippled Helena's banking and commercial houses; Helena would go from six banking establishments in 1892 to just two banks in 1895. The crash would send ripples through Montana's entire economy, severely dislocating large segments of both population and business.

Robert Fisk came to Montana with his brothers in the mid-1860s, and he served as the editor of the *Helena Herald* until the mid-1890s. He died in Berkeley, California, in 1908.

*T*HE *HERALD* will respect its custom of observing the great holiday of Christendom—so this is the last issue of this paper until Tuesday next. Hence we must take advantage of this occasion to wish our readers a "Merry Christmas."

To be sure, it isn't altogether "merry," in the sense of prosperity and hilarity, for some of us. There are many who find the conditions of life less favorable than they were a year ago. No suggestion that partakes of a partisan character should intrude itself at this season. So it can only be said that there has been a change not for the better within the past year in the circumstances of a large part of our population. There are those, as we can bear witness, who have been unaccustomed to manual labor for a long term of years, who now find occasion to turn their hands to a craft almost forgotten.

But is it certain that this is wholly a misfortune? May it not rather be a salutary discipline? If we have been living in a balloon or walking on bubbles, may it not be well that we should plant our feet again upon the solid earth? There is a principle of averages that runs through all human affairs, and sooner or later we are sure to realize it.

There is another fact that may now be borne in upon us with full force of conviction: an abundance of money or physical comforts is not essential to happiness. If we find ourselves restricted in these, as contrasted with other days, there remain the pleasures of the mind that may be catered to by the works of good authors at little cost, and the delights of the family circles that depend only in a slight degree upon what money can buy. He is rather an indifferent specimen of his race whose happiness is measured solely by the money that he has to spend.

Then there is no occasion for down-heartedness. Montana is all right. The clouds will speedily roll by, and the new year that is so fast approaching will not fail to afford its compensations for the deficiencies in the year that is now so nearly spent. In gratitude for the blessings that we enjoy and in the trustful hope of greater ones to come, let us have a Merry Christmas.

Helena Daily Herald, December 23, 1893

Christmas Dinner at the Hotel Helena, 1893

The Hotel Helena was one of the capital city's finest rooming and eating establishments in the early 1890s. Under the direction of Louis A. Walker, the hotel's cuisine was exceptional, given the isolation of the "Queen City of the Rockies" from major population centers.

*E*VER SINCE it has been open, the Christmas dinners at the Hotel Helena have been noted for their excellence. This year Manager Walker has left nothing undone that will insure the keeping up of the good record made in previous years. So, those who do not care to dine at home can go to The Helena, feeling that nowhere else in the city can they get such a Christmas dinner. The menu, as follows, fully proves that:

> Little Neck Clams
> Green Sea Turtle, clear   Consomme, Printaniere Royal
> Salted Almonds   Bouchees à la Reine
> Planked Shad, Beurre
> Potatoes, Duchess

Holiday dinner preparations for the Sixth U.S. Infantry Regiment, Fort Harrison, 1907. Edward M. Reinig, photographer, Montana Historical Society Photograph Archives, Helena

Olives   Celery   Lettuce

Capon with Salt Pork, Anglaise

Frog Saddles, à la Americaine   Game Pie, St. Humbert

Cream Fritters, Curacao Sauce

Prime Rib of Beef   Suckling Pig, Baked Apples

Young Turkey, Chestnut Dressing

Champagne Punch

Roast Partridge, Currant Jelly

Chicken, Mayonnaise   Boned Turkey, Truffles

Mashed Potatoes   Boiled Potatoes

Baked Sweet Potatoes

Asparagus on Toast   French Peas

Cauliflower, à la Creme

[*Christmastime in Montana*   ]

Christmas Pudding, Hard and Brandy Sauce
Mince Pie   Lemon Meringue Pie
Strawberry Bavarian Cream   Maraschino Jelly
Assorted Cake   New York Ice Cream
Confectionery
Nuts   Figs   Raisins   Fruit
Crackers   Edam and American Cheese
Coffee

Helena Daily Independent, December 25, 1893

Death on Christmas Eve, Missoula, 1893

The Christmas holidays have a way of intensifying emotion—either in joy or in sorrow. And no one is immune to these sentiments, regardless of age, station, or location.

ENGINEER HENRY NEFF, one of the oldest employees of the Rocky Mountain Division of the Northern Pacific Railroad, committed suicide at his room in Missoula on Christmas Eve by blowing his brains out with a Winchester rifle.

Livingston Post, December 28, 1893

A Christmas Ball in Livingston, 1893

The railroad and ranching town of Livingston developed a community social life at a slow pace. By the early 1890s, however, in the ongoing effort to achieve respectability, its citizens had graduated to the stage of holding Christmas balls.

THE CHRISTMAS BALL given at Hefferlin Hall by the Young Men's Social and Literary Club was a grand social success. No less than 75 couples participated in the highly enjoyable event.

Friends gathered to celebrate the holiday at Dr. Ben Brooke's residence, 12 S. Benton, Helena, circa 1905. Montana Historical Society Photograph Archives, Helena

The reigning belles were out in force, and they glided through the intricate mazes of the waltz with inimitable grace. The members of the Club took especial pains to make this, their initiatory terpsichorean event, a felicitous one. That they succeeded is vouched for by all those present. Music was furnished by Kumm's orchestra.

Now that the young men composing the Club have demonstrated their ability to provide for the entertainment of the best people of the city who delight to chase the glowing hours with flying feet, their second social dance will be eagerly looked forward to. This, we are informed, will be a masquerade ball to be given in the evening of February 22, Washington's birthday.

Livingston Post, December 28, 1893

The Lumberjacks' Christmas Dinner, 1898

The timber industry in western Montana developed because of the insatiable need for lumber in the Butte mines and the easy freighting offered by the Northern Pacific's mainline. It was called "horse logging," but it required the backbreaking work of thousands of tough men to get the logs out of the forests to the mills. After working long hours, in dangerous conditions, the arrival of Christmas was a welcomed relief for men in these remote lumber camps.

A WESTERN MONTANA logging camp is a cosmopolitan place. The Irishman is there—as he is everywhere. The German is there in his winter garb, looking more Teutonic than a low comedian. The Swede is there, as picturesque as if he had just stepped out of the cast of "Ole Oleson." The Frenchman is there—well represented by the voyageur type, made famous in poetry and fiction. The Englishman is there, as well as the Missourian. Now and then there also is Indian blood evident in some of the men. The American should be mentioned also, but, as in politics, he does not cut much of a figure.

Over all these diverse characters the cook holds sway, and his trusty assistant is the "cookee." At Christmas time, the cook's sovereignty over his subjects becomes more absolute than usual, for every mother's son of a lumberjack looks forward to the observance of that day in the woods. However variant may be the natures of the individuals of the cosmopolitan membership of the crew, there is not one who does not hold in high regard the Christmas holiday.

There is no Christmas tree in the logging camp, and the boys do not hang up their stockings. Sometimes they wish each other a "Merry Christmas," but more often they do not. Their Christmas celebration centers on the dinner. That is why the cook has no difficulty in controlling his sometimes rebellious subjects, as the holiday approaches. The boys want to be sure that he is in good humor, for the better he feels, the better the Christmas dinner will be. This they have learned by experience, and by this experience they profit. To the full extent of their power, they contribute to the success of the dinner, and it is generally a prime one.

There are few city tables that are more heavily laden with good things on Christmas Day than is the long board of the cookhouse at a logging camp. There is a big turkey, of course. More than likely some member of the crew has shot a deer, and the fine, fat saddle of the venison graces the Christmas table. Cranberries have been brought from town, as well as fruit and nuts. There are steaming dishes of vegetables, and there are long rows of pies. There is a big pudding, too, if the cook has been feeling right. The bill of fare is one that would do credit to a big hotel, for these camp cooks are experts and, when they make an effort, the result is sure to be a success.

There is not much style about the boarding department of the average logging camp, but it is clean and the food is abundant and wholesome. There is no lack of appetite either, on the part of the regular boarders. A half-day's work in the timber, with snow a foot or more deep, is calculated to put a good appetite into the frame of almost any man. Add to this normal condition of hollowness, the zest that is afforded by anticipation of the delights of the Christmas dinner and by the spirit of the glad season, and the condition of the lumberjack at dinner time on Christmas Day may be easily imagined.

Outside the door of the cookhouse is suspended a broken circular saw that has been brought up from the mill. The equipment of no logging camp is complete without this. When dinner is ready, the "cookee" pounds away on this saw with a club, and the resulting sound is one that makes a Chinese gong ashamed of itself. It penetrates to the uttermost parts of the forest, and it is sweet music to the hungry toilers in the woods. On Christmas, at dinner time, this tocsin rings out with a more pronounced tone than usual. It discounts in volume and penetrating power any chime of church or cathedral that ever announced the advent of Christmas Day.

Out through the snow-covered forest, the cadence of its music rises and falls. It sets the crisp, sharp air all aquiver and rattles the snow from the branches of fir and pine. It wakes the echoes for miles around and sends the startled deer scampering to cover. It tells the lumberjack that his Christmas dinner is ready, and he right cheerfully responds to its summons.

The long dining room of the cookhouse looks its best as the lumberjack enters. Everything is shiny. The tin and earthen dishes have been polished and the floor is bright. The rough log walls seem to beam with good cheer, and the big box stove in the middle of the room sends a warm greeting to the hungry jacks as they come trooping in. The "cookee" beams from the kitchen door, and from that room are wafted the savory odors of the good things that are being prepared for the table by the cook. This master rattles away among his pans and kettles, hurrying to be ready for the horde of hungry fellows who will soon demolish the substantial repast that is coming up.

Quickly each man takes his place on one of the long benches that extend along the sides of the table. The crowd is merry and noisy. Jokes and keen retorts fly back and forth, and the "cookee" comes in for his share of the good-natured chaff. With a final scrape and shuffle, the benches are drawn close to the tables, comparative silence prevails, and decks are cleared for action.

The "cookee" rushes along the tables, placing the dishes of potatoes, cranberry sauce, and other accompaniments of the turkey. This does not take much time. Everything is soon ready for the big thing, and the "cookee"

Santa Claus and townsfolk pose in front of Sidney's Yellowstone Mercantile, the store that declared itself "The Christmas Store," circa 1906. Montana Historical Society Photograph Archives, Helena

brings in the turkeys. Big and brown and fragrant they are and, if anything were needed to whet the appetites of the men along the tables, it would be the savory odors that exhale from the national bird. The turkeys are placed upon the table and the feast is on. The Christmas of the lumberjack in Western Montana is in full celebration.

Anaconda Standard, December 17, 1899

First Christmas in Jardine, 1899

The settlement of Jardine in Bear Gulch is located above Gardiner, just north of Yellowstone National Park. Although Bear Gulch had supported several small mining operations, large-scale development was brought by Harry Bush in 1899. Despite this Englishman's vision, though, the Revenue Mining Company failed in 1906. Bear Gulch has been mined intermittently during the last nine decades, by various means.

*T*HERE WAS JOY at Jardine on Christmas Day, and the holiday was celebrated with a feeling of exuberance which well might be felt for years by both the residents of the camp and those in charge of the operations there.

It was not so long ago that there was no Jardine at all. Bear Gulch was there—and the gulch was all there was to it. It is not much more than one year ago when there was only a few prospect holes where now exist the splendidly developed mines called the Revenue, the Sowash, the Legal Tender, and many others.

A little over a twelvemonth ago, a few shacks occupied the places were now stand substantial structures of stone and lumber. Where the prospector crushed the grudging granite in his mortar and washed the gold in sparse quantities from out the rock, the stamp mills are ever grinding their grist of wealth, and the busy hum of buzzing belts is heard anon. It was indeed a fitting time for a celebration, and the affair which occurred at Jardine on Christmas has had no equal in the social annals of Park County. And it is doubtful if the State of Montana has ever witnessed a banquet of more dazzling brilliancy or greater magnitude.

As they did in this 1887 photograph, winter visitors still make tracks in the timeless Upper Geyser Basin of Yellowstone National Park. F. Jay Haynes, photographer, Haynes Foundation Collection, Montana Historical Society Photograph Archives, Helena

It has been under the management of Harry Bush that these marvelous improvements have been made, and this gentleman resolved to give Jardine a Christmas which would linger in the minds of those who attended for years. Accordingly, arrangements were made for a grand banquet in the Revenue Mill on Christmas Day. Mrs. Bush was given charge of the arrangements, and the success which attended the affair is a splendid commentary upon the ability of Mrs. Bush as an entertainer and is a fact showing that Harry Bush is not the only person in Bear Gulch who makes no mistakes in laying plans.

The scene of the banquet was the machine shop of the Revenue Mill, the room being vacant on account of the machinery not yet having arrived. The room was decorated in a manner that rendered it a perfect bower of loveliness. The roof was a solid bank of evergreens, dotted here and there with electric lights of various hues. Bunting of national colors swung in graceful folds around the room, and the most exquisite cut flowers lent their delightful perfume and beauty to the scene.

The tables were laid for 100 persons and were profusely decorated with cut flowers and ferns, and they presented a most artistic appearance. At 6 o'clock the banquet began, and it was 10 o'clock before the guests who had assembled to enjoy the hospitality of Mr. and Mrs. Bush had regaled themselves at the festive board. The menu abounded in delicacies, and every luxury in the line of edibles that could be found in the market graced the tables.

As a reminder of early days in Montana, a buffalo had been purchased by Mr. Bush. The juicy steaks and tender roasts of the monarch of the plains in days gone by contributed a share of the feast. Elk and deer, fowl of every description, and products of the salt seas and of the clear waters of the Yellowstone River were there in generous abundance. The best of everything was none too good for the guest assembled at the banquet, and it is safe to say that no greater enjoyment was ever had by any crowd than was furnished Christmas Day to the assemblage at Jardine.

After the banquet was over, the rooms were cleared and the guests formed on the floor for the grand march. An orchestra of eleven pieces furnished music for the promenade and, as the first strains of the grand march swelled forth, the entire machinery of the Revenue Mill was set in gentle motion. Mr. and Mrs. Harry Bush led the march and, to the dropping of the stamps, the host of guests were conducted through every floor of the vast structure, winding about the various rooms until the starting point was again reached; then a quadrille was formed.

The remainder of the evening was most pleasantly spent, and the breaking up of the assembly marked the close of the greatest social event ever held in Montana. It was a day to be long remembered and looked back upon in pleasant retrospect throughout the lives of those who attended.

Too much credit cannot be given Mrs. Bush for the able manner in which she conducted the arrangements and carried out every plan, even to the smallest details. Nothing was lacking to make the banquet all that it was intended to be—and a remarkable foresight was exercised by Mrs. Bush in superintending the affair.

Those in attendance came from various parts in the Upper Yellowstone and, in fact, from all over Montana. The men employed in the properties of Mr. Bush were the guests of honor and were shown every attention throughout the progress of the banquet, as indeed were all those present. Christmas Day was a truly great day for Jardine!

Livingston Post, December 28, 1899

Christmas Preparations for the Poor of Butte, 1899

In the late 1890s, Butte came as close to resembling an Eastern, urban center as Montana could offer. It is not surprising, then, that the people of Butte pioneered the organizational celebration of Christmas for the city's poor residents. With the help of a generous citizenry, the Associated Charities of Butte provided much-needed assistance to the city's multi-national population.

*I*N THIS HAPPY Christmas season, the poor of Butte will not be overlooked. Few cities are more prosperous than is Butte; few cities have greater reason to be thankful than has Butte; in few cities is there less real poverty and distress. Yet Butte has its poor, and these poor will not be forgotten during the holiday season. Santa Claus is going to visit the homes of the poor.

The ladies who are engaged in the noble work of the Associated Charities of Butte intend that no poor children shall be forgotten this year in this city, and that no poor families shall be without a good dinner on Christmas Day. They want the whole city to be happy on the anniversary of the birth of Christ. If their plans are successfully carried through, every poor family will have something to be thankful for.

Boys sledding in front of R. T. Smith home, Pony. Montana Historical Society Photograph Archives, Helena

In the first place, the ladies of the association will send this week a load of coal to every poor family. A year ago Marcus Daly gave the association 200 tons of coal for the poor of Butte. Much of this coal is still on hand and will be distributed at this appropriate time.

Then, in the second place, the association proposes to give each poor family a Christmas dinner. The same plan adopted last Christmas is to be followed. The association asks that all the people of Butte who feel able to do so furnish some poor family a Christmas dinner. It is not asked that the dinner be prepared, but only that the materials be furnished.

Everyone who is disposed to help gladden Christmas among Butte's poor is requested to notify the association, either by letter addressed to the association's headquarters in the Library building, or by calling there in person.

The Associated Charities is preparing a list of the worthy poor families, and the work of distributing Christmas comforts will be carried through in a systematic manner. Those who prefer can send to the association, in lieu of the materials for a dinner, the money with which the dinner fixings can be bought. It was in this way that the worthy poor families were provided with dinners last year. It is hoped that equal success will attend this year's endeavors.

The third part of the work of the association is directed toward getting up the most glorious kind of a Christmas tree for the poor children. The day for the Christmas tree has not yet been set. It is intended that all the children shall receive a Christmas gift. In order that they may be successful in this plan, the ladies ask for donations of toys, picture books, and gifts of all kinds from both merchants and others who have them to give.

It will take a great many presents to go around, and the charitable people of Butte cannot be too liberal in this matter. Every merchant will have toys on hand that he will not care to keep in stock another year, and every wealthy family has more toys than are needed by the children of the family. The rich children would never miss the toys, and they would make the holiday season brighter for many poor children.

These are the plans of the ladies of the Associated Charities for making all Butte happy at Christmastide. The ladies have never yet failed to consummate their plans, and the consummation this year means that all Butte's poor will have reason to be happy.

The lot of the poor in Butte has indeed been happier since the Associated Charities was organized two years ago. The organization has become of inestimable benefit to the poor. It is the only organized effort in the city for the distribution of charity. Its principle is to help the poor to help themselves, and it has been eminently successful in this work.

Anaconda Standard, December 17, 1899

A Trapper's Old-Time Christmas, 1900

To Montanans celebrating the holidays in town, the thought of spending Christmas Day in an isolated mountain cabin lacked appeal. However, hundreds of trappers at the turn of the century looked forward to a special Christmas—one replete with traditions they had developed through the years in isolation. Such was the case with John Burns, who invited Dan Dougall to spend the Christmas of 1900 with him.

TWO VETERAN MOUNTAINEERS, Dan Dougall and John Burns, from Blacktail Canyon, came to town yesterday afternoon. They wore leggings made of burlap, and they wore unplucked beaver caps; they smoked pipes strong enough to raise the price of silver.

They spent the day in the back room of a cozy, warm cigar store and, to while the hours away, they joined a few friends in a game of "freezeout" for the cigars.

John and Dan have piled up a little money during the summer, and they propose to spend a few dollars on an old-time Christmas. They will return to their mountain home today with sow-belly, New Orleans molasses, yeast powders, dried apples and raisins, tobacco, whiskey, nuts, and a new deck of cards.

"I have not eaten a Christmas dinner in town since I left the Ohio Valley," said Mr. Burns, "and that has been 31 years. Every Christmas I fix up a dinner in the old cabin, and you bet I enjoy it. That is one day in the 365 when the old black cabin looks like home to me. I have never forgotten how nice the house used to look on Christmas when I was a boy at home. We children never went away from home to spend Christmas. I have learned to regard home with a sort of childlike reverence, and therefore I don't want to stay in Butte over Christmas Day.

"I have invited Dan to eat with me, and we will have a spread that won't be duplicated anywhere in Butte. I am going to try to get up a dinner like I cooked the first winter I spent in Montana in 1869. I was in Bannack and had a lot of dried apples and raisins that I brought from the East with me. I had sow-belly and molasses, and a jug of good whiskey. I am going to get up a similar bill of fare, and I'll bet it's a bird of a feast, too."

Dan Dougall has not been in Montana quite so many years as his partner, but he has smiled away 27 cold Montana winters. He usually comes to town to spend Christmas.

"This time I'm going to be good," said Dan. "It has been my custom to come to town and fill up with Tom and Jerry and smoke. Now I'm going to eat an old-fashioned dinner, and spend the evening playing 'casino' for the drinks with John."

Anaconda Standard, December 24, 1900

Hans Oleson's Strange Christmas Present, Butte, 1900

The time-honored practice of making a Christmas gift for a loved one can be carried to an extreme, as Hans Oleson discovered. He worked, both before and after this incident, as a laborer at the Colorado Smelter in Butte.

*Y*ESTERDAY a young Swede named Hans Oleson was compelled to leave his rooming apartment on West Quartz Street because he was suspected of being a dangerous person to have about the place. It appears that Hans was affectionately engaged upon the construction of a Christmas gift for his flaxen-haired sweetheart, and the racket he made during his operations so annoyed the other roomers in the dwelling that they complained to the land-lady of the place and had Hans served with a notice to quit.

The contrivance that Hans was devising for the purpose of winning the good graces of the winsome young lady with whom he was infatuated is a

Homestead of Mrs. John Paulley near Valier, January 15, 1909. Montana Historical Society Photograph Archives, Helena

ingenious one. It consists of a rough board upon which was fastened a toy pistol, and the deadly barrel of this terrible weapon was directed toward a hugh red heart, arranged in the position of a target for the miniature cannon.

Beneath the roughly fashioned machine for harvesting the affections of his sweetheart, Hans had crudely traced a few lines of poetry in his native language. The inspired composition was to the effect that the tender glances his lady love shot at him were puncturing his heart in the same effective way that the double-barreled pistol was supposed to riddle the ventricles of the red target. The pistol was fitted with caps and designed to fire as the cover of the box containing the unique toy was lifted. It was the exploding caps fired by Hans in testing the mechanism of his novel present that roused the ire of the roomers adjacent to his workshop.

Hans left the peculiar toy behind him when he went away, and the roomers at the place have had all kinds of fun with the cast-off Christmas gift.

Anaconda Standard, December 16, 1900

A Christmas Message from
Rev. Edward Oliver Tilburn, 1900

After graduating from Yale University in 1881, Edward Oliver Tilburn pursued an acting career and wrote numerous plays for the New York stage. He travelled the world as a thespian and organized his own acting company with which he toured the United States. He also worked as a lead editor for Chicago publishing houses before converting to evangelical Christianity and obtaining a graduate degree in theology. The Reverend Tilburn served the Shortridge Memorial Christian Church in Butte beginning in 1899.

*D*URING THE French Revolution, a priest was confined to one of the dungeons of a well-known prison in Paris. A narrow slit in the masonry served the purpose of a window. It admitted all the light by which the occupant of the unpleasant quarters could distinguish the day from the night. Here the good man died.

Interior of Fort Benton's old Catholic Church decorated for Christmas, 1891. Montana Historical Society Photograph Archives, Helena

After his death, some words were found scratched on the wall above, below, and on either side of the window. Above was written "Height"; below "Depth"; on one side "Length"; on the other side "Breadth." And under all of the markings was written "Light, Love, and Fullness of God." The window was small, but through it came all the light that the priest had enjoyed. To him it was the measure of the fullness of love, even as it was the measure of the fullness of light.

Christmas is the time of gifts. It memorializes the gift of God in Jesus our Lord. While it is extremely doubtful that the Christ child saw the light of day upon the date we celebrate His natal day, yet the fact of His birth is commemorated. With that also comes the recognition that God kept his promises to Abraham and Isaac and Jacob, and that the prophecies concerning One who would come in love to rule the world were fulfilled.

With the coming of the glad day of "Peace on earth, and good will toward men," we are constrained to give "Glory to God in the highest!" For, if we through love bestow gifts upon the objects of our affection or esteem, surely it was a greater evidence of love that led to the sending to earth the "Light of the World." Indeed, "God so loved the world that He gave His only begotten Son"—and gave Him to a world which loved Him not, nor esteemed His mission.

With the thought of the meaning of the Christmastime should also come sufficient light to enable us to write on the walls of our earthly abiding place "The height of God's love is even to the heavens. The depth is even to the lowest places of sin and depravity. The length of God's love is as far as the world shall reach. The breadth covers all that He has made."

This is the fullness of God. "He that spared not His own Son, but delivered Him up for us all—how shall He not also freely give us all things?"

Anaconda Standard, December 16, 1900

Christmas in the Deer Lodge County Jail, 1900

John Conley was the brother of Frank, long-time warden at the Montana State Prison. John came to Montana in the 1870s as a U.S. Army packer during a period of tumultuous relations with the Lakotas and Cheyennes. He served as a deputy sheriff in Miles City, Livingston, and Glendive before coming to Anaconda in 1885. In 1898 he was elected the sheriff of Deer Lodge County, and to this position he brought an unusual amount of experience. John Conley's Christmas spirit extended to his wards, the prisoners in the Deer Lodge County Jail.

*T*HE 28 PRISONERS in the County Jail will enjoy a sumptuous turkey dinner today at 12 o'clock. Ever since Sheriff Conley has been in office, it has been one of his fads that, on Christmas Day, when all is cheerful, the inmates of the County Jail shall fare as well as their more fortunate fellowmen on the outside.

To that end, there was delivered at the doors of the county stronghold yesterday 100 pounds of the finest turkey meat it is possible to buy. Accompanying this nucleus of a Christmas feast were cranberries galore—to be made into pies and sauce—and mince meat in large buckets, which is nearly as necessary to the enjoyment of the yearly blowout as turkey.

The dinner will not be served as late in the day as it is in more fashionable circles, but it will be, for all that, fully as well enjoyed. It has been said that some of the hardened wretches within the prison walls were not deserving of such kindness, but it is certain that on Christmas, the holiest day of the year, the stoniest and most unsympathetic heart in the world is touched to some extent.

Strange as it may seem, the good predominates in all classes at this sacred time, and those doing time are more grateful for the good things tendered them at Yuletide than at any other time of the year. At this time, everybody gives, everybody receives, and all should be peace on earth, good will toward men.

This is the view that Sheriff Conley takes of the matter and, because of this, the prisoners of Deer Lodge County will have a "feed" today that they will remember during the years to come.

Anaconda Standard, December 25, 1900

A Huge Christmas Celebration in Anaconda, 1900

"Copper King" Marcus Daly created the town of Anaconda in 1883 to serve as the site of his copper-ore smelting operations. Although it always existed in the shadow of Butte (30 miles to the east), Anaconda sported 9,500 people in 1900 and some civic activities typically associated with a metropolis. The Elks who organized and conducted this mass community celebration would have been welcome in a city ten times Anaconda's size.

*M*ORE THAN 3,000 children were the guests of the Benevolent and Protective Order of Elks yesterday at Turner Hall.

That was a Christmas festival on a grand scale. Children of rich and poor, children who had plenty, but wanted just some little remembrance from the real, live, sure-enough Santa Claus, and children whose only Christmas joy would be tasted in that big, crowded hall, were all there.

To rich and poor the same open-handed Christmas greeting was extended:

> At Christmas play, and make good cheer.
> For Christmas comes but once a year.

The making of 3,000 children happy, if only for one day, is something worthy of the efforts of the greatest and most powerful men. With no self-glorification, modestly and systematically, the Elks undertook the task and made it a success. The expense, in proportion to the amount of happiness dispensed, was small. The thought came to many who looked on that gay scene that it was odd that no one in this part of the country every before thought of the plan that produced so much for such a small investment. The expense is numbered in hundreds of dollars, the results in thousands of happy hearts.

True it is that some of the children who enjoyed the festivities really needed not this extra Christmas, but think of the hundreds to whom it meant much.

The great tree, a stately pine, whose length had to be reduced to get it into the hall, occupied the center of the great apartment. Its tip touched the ceiling, 24 feet above the floor. Never was there such a Christmas tree before in

Anaconda. The artistic skill of the lodge—for all members threw themselves, heart and soul, into the work—was expended in its decoration. Brilliant beyond words, it awed the children with its beauty. They were amazed, struck dumb by admiration.

Tinsel and glittering toys caught and reflected the many lights. Dolls and drums and horns and toy animals peeped from the maze of branches. One hundred brilliant electric globes, their wires cleverly concealed, blazed forth from the boughs. Twelve hundred feet of purple and white paper decorations hung festooned on the tree. The purple and whitebound supports were almost hidden under the cartload after cartload of presents that were stacked about.

The whole hall came in for elaborate decorations. Five thousand feet of bunting were used in this work with pleasing effect.

To keep back the crowd, a square surrounding the tree was roped off. Outside this a way was kept open around the ropes by Elks who patrolled up and down, caring for the children and preventing a crush. The Elks wore streamers of purple and white, and they bore upon their heads their white and purple caps.

Four o'clock was the hour set for the opening, but before that time the hall was filled. Mothers and big sisters, fathers and big brothers were there, escorting the wide-eyed little ones. There were closely huddled groups of little girls, while the gaps in the crowd were filled by the independent, eager small boys.

At length the larger boys were induced to go up stairs, and there they quickly filled the galleries. The Margaret Theater orchestra, stationed on the stage, had been playing its choicest selections, and now it struck up a lively cakewalk.

"Here comes Santa Claus!" rose the cry. And, from the front of the hall, good old Saint Nicholas himself bounded into the crowd and, gaily smiling, tripped around the way left open for him—shaking hands with the children as he passed. He wore his gayest costume for the occasion, a blue fur-trimmed suit, upon which a score or more bells tinkled as he moved. His rosy face and white beard were all the storybooks have pictured.

As he passed along, some of the older children who want to be thought pessimistic declared that Santa Claus looked an awful lot like R. de R. Smith in disguise, but the younger ones knew better. Their faith was not to be shaken by any such absurd and manifestly untrue statements.

And then Santa leaped inside the roped-off square, followed by the Elks themselves, and the distribution began. Well it was that the Elks had the protection of the ropes, else they would have been engulfed in the sea of a small humanity that swept treeward.

Some effort at systematic distribution was made, but the system would not work to perfection. No system could, and it was lots more fun to have it unsystematic, after all. The attempt was made to have the children pass around the roped square, receive the good things Santa Claus gave, and then go on out the side door. It was accomplished in a sort of a way.

Of course, the smaller children, those on the floor, were served first. A bit of strategy had been executed, and a force of stalwart Elks guarded the stairway to hold the larger youngsters in the gallery. These guardian Elks had a busy time. Try to keep a thousand or more boys from coming down stairs when they are frantic to get down, and see if you have any time for profound thought while so engaged.

Good-natured Elks about the tree tossed bags of candy and nuts, apples and oranges into the gallery to hold the boys for a while.

Santa Claus and his assistants gave to the passing children 2,500 generous packages of candy and nuts, 3,000 apples, 3,000 oranges, and several thousand Christmas cards. These latter gifts were for the little girls, but some of the boys got them too.

This supply was passed out in very short time. The behavior of the children was admirable. There was less crowding than one

Duncan George McDonald at age two, 1890. Montana Historical Society Photograph Archives, Helena

would expect, and the larger boys were allowed down from the galleries in ample time to get their shares.

In an hour and a half, the greater crowd had been satisfied, but from then on to 8 o'clock children were coming and going all the time, and none went away without something. The 20 dozen popcorn balls, the 2,000 feet of strung cranberries, and the 2,000 feet of strung popcorn on the tree all were used up.

In such a crowd, it would have been impossible to give out presents judiciously, so Santa Claus explained that the presents would be distributed by wagon today. Lists of deserving children who have been good during the year have been made up.

As the first excitement subsided, the children waylaid Santa Claus and whispered their requests. "Bring me a doll, Santa," would be the request of a little maid, while her sturdy brother would whisper excitedly, "Say, bring me a sled, won't you?"

Of course there were some repeaters—youngsters who would stuff their bags of candy under their coats and come back for more, but these were few.

Garnet, 1898. Montana Historical Society Photograph Archives, Helena

It would be hard to find a better behaved lot of children anywhere. Good home bringing-up was manifest in many.

An Elk, holding in his hand a bunch of pretty Christmas cards, would ask a little girl if she had received a card. Instantly she would answer in the affirmative, though her eyes would linger longingly on the bunch. Many were those instances. They more than atoned for the more selfish attitude of the very small minority of small boys and girls and their mammas who tried to repeat, even at the risk of depriving some worthy child.

During the hours the tree was on exhibition and the distribution was in progress, the Margaret Theater orchestra rendered a number of selections. Douglas Smith also contributed to the entertainment by singing several solos.

Anaconda Standard, December 25, 1900

Mrs. Ford's Christmas Menu, Great Falls, 1902

Sue McClanahan married Robert Simpson Ford in Kentucky in 1878 and came to live on his Sun River ranch. She was the daughter of a distinguished, old Kentucky family. The Fords moved into Great Falls in 1892, where Mrs. Ford became a stalwart of the town's social and charitable projects. Her death in 1906 was sincerely mourned by the population of Great Falls.

*P*ERHAPS NO Great Falls woman has been more highly complimented for her numerous successes as a hostess than has Mrs. Robert S. Ford. When the *Tribune* asked her to recommend to the many women who will read this Christmas number a choice menu for Christmas dinner, it was with confidence that the result would be most pleasing. In gracious compliance with our request, Mrs. Ford has outlined the following menu as one that she would consider most suitable if she were to give a Christmas dinner:

First course—Grape fruit, served with red cherries.

Second course—Blue Point oysters, served on the half shell with lemon baskets and celery.

Third course—Chicken consomme, with whipped cream, having red sugar sprinkled on top. Soup straws.

Fourth course—Creamed lobster, in red paper cases, with trouffles; or, macaroni, served with timbales.

Fifth course—Fried sweetbreads, with green peas; or, steamed mushrooms on toast.

Sixth course—Turkey cutlets, red paper frills, sweet potatoes, croquettes, currant or cranberry jelly, hot rolls, tied with red bebe ribbon, and chocolate.

Seventh course—Beet salad, served on green leaves (made of any kind of preferred salad, served in large scooped beet, with mayonnaise; the top of beet trimmed with vegetable scissors and replaced).

Eighth course—Ice cream, served in the form and color of an American Beauty rose; small cakes, with red icing.

Ninth course—Bonbons and fruits, in red and green (on table).

Tenth course—Coffee in the drawing room.

Mrs. Ford gave a beautifully appointed Christmas dinner for 16 persons last year, and the above menu is the refinement of that social engagement.

Great Falls Tribune, December 21, 1902

Christmas Business in Missoula, 1908

Because of a brief national financial crisis in 1907, business closely watched the Christmas buying season of 1908 hoping to see indications of an economic rebound. In Missoula that recovery proved particularly successful. Moreover, after the turn of the century, businessmen began to realize the importance of Christmas sales to their annual profits.

*W*ITH A RUSH and a jam, Missoula's 10 days of Christmas shopping came to a reluctant but brilliant finish with the closing of the business houses here late tonight. When the doors closed, there were still many late shoppers yet to be waited upon. And the tired clerks gave a sigh of relief when the last customer had been escorted to the door, near the midnight hour.

The Christmas trade has been exceptionally successful from every point of view in the Garden City this year. The stores were first of all supplied with goods of such quality and variable nature that the most eccentric buyer could

Snow piled up to the horse's belly during Dupuyer's snowstorm of October 10–14, 1899.
Montana Historical Society Photograph Archives, Helena

find just what he was looking for. Then, from the merchants' standpoint, there were more shoppers than ever before, and they all had money and were anxious to spend it at home.

From the preparations everywhere in evidence today, Christmas will be an unusually happy occasion and generally observed in every home. And, when Santa Claus begins the work of distributing presents, it will be from a pack of immense proportions. The result will be that stockings will be filled, and Christmas trees and chimney corners will be heavily laden with presents when the children—and the old people too—awake tomorrow.

The holiday spirit is everywhere contagious, and the happy salutations and exchanges of the season's greetings are heard on every hand. Missoula has just passed through her most prosperous and successful year. And it is safe to say that Christmas will be one of the happiest and merriest in the city's history.

Anaconda Standard, December 25, 1908

First Christmas on Iowa Bench, 1908

The Iowa Bench area is located about 25 miles northwest of Lewistown. The Gladsons were pioneer homesteaders in that area at the turn of the century. In 1958, when she wrote this piece, Mrs. Gladson was more than 80 years old and had retired near Denton. Her account of a homestead Christmas typifies the strong sense of community created by holidays, even when confronted with isolation and an extremely harsh climate.

*T*HE FIRST Christmas-tree celebration and Christmas program ever held on the Iowa Bench, south of the present town of Denton, was held in the homestead cabin of Mr. and Mrs. Charlie Gladson on December, 1908. The cabin's dimensions were 14 by 22 feet—not much room, but Charlie and I decided to have a Christmas tree and to invite in the Iowa Bench people that homesteaded there. It was our first Christmas on our homestead, and we wanted to share it with others.

Children skiing in Yellowstone National Park, 1894. F. Jay Haynes, photographer, Haynes Foundation Collection, Montana Historical Society Photograph Archives, Helena

We drove around to the homes and invited them to come. And we also told them that they were welcome to cooperate with us, if they wished to, which they did gladly. The women and children got busy making various presents and trimmings for the tree, and the menfolk also made presents. Charlie made a little doll table and I made a tablecloth for it, using a lace medallion off my wedding dress for a centerpiece.

Then Charlie made a very pretty doll cart, using a date basket for the body, and a pair of my embroidery hoops as the wheels. Then together we made a child's doll cupboard, chairs, and davenport. I made silk neckties for the little boys.

The rest of the homesteaders were just as busy, working with a zest to make the tree a success and a happy event. Charlie and I drove to Stanford to get the candy, nuts, oranges, and apples—also a few little candies for the tree—which was a journey of 50 miles with team and buggy, at ten below zero.

Just north and a little west of us lived Jake and Chris Knerr and their niece and her two children. We invited them. The children had never seen a Christmas tree or Santa Claus. They asked their Uncle Jake, "Which way will Santa come?" And he told them, "Right over Square Butte, and he will land on the school section right by the Gladson's house."

On the day before Christmas, we put everything we could in the cave we had dug near the house for storage, leaving only the stove, chairs, davenport, and organ. Our bed was a set of springs hinged to the wall, so it would fold up to the wall and under a deep shelf. Thus folded, it took up very little space. So we did not have to put our bed out-of-doors.

We placed the tree in the corner of the room, and we made a mock fireplace by its side. The children put on a nice program of songs and readings, and a play called "Spies on Santy." Little Charlie Gladson (a very chubby boy) was Santy, and Mary Gladson and Ray Johnston were the spies. They each got a pillowslip and hung it on the fireplace mantle, but both fell asleep.

Next on the program was singing "Jingle Bells," as I accompanied them on the organ. Just as we finished singing, we heard Santa's sleighbells as he drove up to the house. Bill Hill was Santa and Dave Mason was Mrs. Santa. "She" said that "she" had to come along to help Santa drive, because the

Montana jackrabbits were so large that the reindeer got confused. They thought that the rabbits were deer and wanted to play with them.

After the gifts were removed from the tree, a lunch was served of ham sandwiches, doughnuts, coffee, and popcorn balls for every one present.

I still live on that same homestead alone. My husband, the late Charlie Gladson, built our larger home over 30 years ago. We enjoyed it together, until his passing in the late 1930s.

At that first Christmas party, there were 35 people in all. The lunch was prepared at the Grandpa and Grandma Holgates' cabin, which was not very far from ours. What a wonderful Christmas this all was for our first Christmas in Montana, on the homestead.

Lewistown Daily News, December 21, 1958

Plentywood's First Christmas Tree Celebration, 1909

The high plains of eastern Montana, which had served stockmen since the 1870s, began to assume a different look when homesteaders moved in after 1906. In Plentywood, 50 miles north of Culbertson, those homesteaders brought Christmas traditions with them and transplanted them in new soil. And it is more than coincidence that the Great Northern Railway's branch line reached this promising young town in 1910.

*C*HRISTMAS DAY has come and gone. All that remains are the pleasant memories of a merry time. And certainly the testimony is not conflicting in and around Plentywood on the last point. Everyone we have had a chance to interrogate has expressed himself in no discordant language that the first public celebration of a Christmas tree in our little burg was a pronounced success.

We cannot desist from expressing our own opinion that we have been eye-witness to a goodly number of Christmas-tree celebrations before. But the one—and be it said the first one at Plentywood, Montana, and vicinity—eclipsed any thing we have ever witnessed before. The ladies who planned it are to be complimented, as well as all those who responded so willingly and liberally when called upon in a financial way. Those who participated in the exercises, as well as those who were instrumental in planning them, are to be congratulated.

From everyone we note expressions of surprise that the programme could have been so artistically arranged, the stage so beautifully decorated, and those who carried out the programme so excellent in its rendition. At no time was there the least monotony, for the elements productive of monotony were lacking, and every one was anxious to see if the next number could excel the one preceding it.

Indeed, Plentywood has ample reasons to be proud. Situated 54 miles from the nearest railway town and being able to accomplish this feat deserves to be recorded for future reference. Our first Christmas tree will bring pleasant memories for years to come.

Plentywood Herald, December 31, 1909

Agriculture and Tough Times

*D*URING MONTANA's first twentieth-century decades, hordes of homesteaders settled the high plains and western forests. The homestead boom (1908–1917) changed the composition of the state's population, spurred a wave of Progressive politics, and popularized such new technologies as automobiles, telephones, and radios. Unfortunately, an agricultural bust (1918–1938) crippled Montana's economy. Montanans barely acknowledged the arrival of the Great Depression in the early 1930s, since they already had suffered for more than a decade!

During these tough times, Christmas celebrations helped sustain Montana homes and culture. The holidays took on real economic clout, towns instituted community-wide Christmas activities, and a reliance on institutional and government-agency charity became more acceptable. What was lost in abundance was gained in spirit. Montanans simply learned to adapt . . . again.

Feeding cattle by sleigh on the Willard Ranch near Augusta circa 1930. Montana Historical Society Photograph Archives, Helena

Japanese Christmas Festival, Deer Lodge, 1910

The settlement of Montana by European and Asian ethnic groups was most pronounced around the turn of the century. When immigrant families and groups preserved homeland customs, they created a rich fabric for the celebration of the winter solstice. A variation on this ethnic theme occurred at St. James Episcopal Church in Deer Lodge, shortly after the Christmas of 1910. The Japanese population in Montana at this time was almost 1,600 people.

O̶N̶ WEDNESDAY, December 28, 1910, the Christmas festival of the Japanese took place in St. James's Church in this city. A large number of printed invitations had been sent out, and quite a large gathering of friends was there to greet the 25 or more Japanese who gathered to enjoy the services, and also to make their visitors happy.

The hymns were in English, but most of the service (that of shortened evening prayer) was in Japanese. The service was conducted by Paul J.

Mrs. Rose Drew Paulley's Christmas dinner party at Lavina, 1938. Montana Historical Society Photograph Archives, Helena

Tajima, who also translated into Japanese a short address given by the Rev. W. J. Attwood. The features of the evening were the addresses of welcome by Mr. Tajima and the distribution of gifts by the Japanese.

A large number of valuable Japanese articles, as presents, had been prepared—as well as candy, nuts, and oranges for the children. In the order of the choir, the Sunday School teachers and scholars, the congregation, the friends of the Japanese, and the Japanese themselves the various remembrances were given out, amid many expressions of surprise and delight.

After the closing hymn, many expressed their appreciation to the Japanese for what was a most enjoyable Christmas festival.

Deer Lodge Silver State Post, January 4, 1911

Christmas in a New House, 1910

In 1908 Edna Patterson's parents brought their five children to a homestead claim nine miles north of Intake, a small community about 15 miles down the Yellowstone River from Glendive, in Dawson County. In these excerpts from an oral-history interview, Edna tells of the family's first Christmas in their new frame house on the claim.

*W*E MOVED into our new house on the homestead on the 23rd of December, 1910. . . . We then went with the horse and buggy, and the ax, and we were going to get a cedar tree for Christmas. We went up about a half a mile or more from the house, and we found two little cedar trees in the coulee. That's all we found. They were too precious to cut for our Christmas tree, so we cut down a bullberry bush, and we took it home.

Mother had a couple newspapers that she had packed around dishes and things. She let us cut them up into little strips, and she made us some flour paste. We made those strips all into chains, paper chains. Then we decorated the bullberry bush with the chains. It was a sight to behold, I'll tell you. Daddy put a board across the bottom of it, so it would stand up. We had some crayons that we had brought from Iowa with us—some color crayons—so we colored some of those pieces of paper and made them into paper chains.

. . . For Christmas dinner, Mother had put this big prairie chicken pie in the oven to bake. And she had baked cookies the day before, so there were lots of cookies. I can't remember what they were like, but they had strings in them, so you could hang them on the Christmas tree. . . . Mother and Daddy had coffee with the chicken pie dinner, I can remember that. . . . That was our first Christmas dinner in the homestead house.

Edna Patterson,
interview by Laurie Mercier, Glendive, Mont.,
October 26, 29, 1981, Oral History 205,
Montanans at Work Oral History Project,
Montana Historical Society Archives, Helena

Christmas at Avon, 1910

In 1910 Christmas Day fell on a Sunday, so the residents of Avon in Powell County joined with the telephone-line construction workers to celebrate a "Christmas Eve" holiday on Friday evening. Mrs. Louquet's "domino" was a long, loose cloak, with a hood and wide sleeves.

𝓕RIDAY NIGHT was the big "Christmas Eve" in Avon, to avoid breaking over into the Sabbath. The school children, aided by the Avon Telephone Company's construction crew, gave a Christmas-tree entertainment. The children gave a number of splendid recitations in a most pleasing, natural, and child-like manner; the Mead Orchestra rendered several numbers of sacred and other music, appropriate to the occasion, in a most satisfactory manner. The affair was very successful, and it was highly appreciated by all present.

There were two large trees, glittering with bright ornaments and underlaid with piles of presents for all. Much credit is due the ladies who carried it through, in the face of what appeared to be overwhelming obstacles. The "Christmas spirit" is a poor make-shift when it fails to bring Santa Claus to the children at this particular time. What is Christianity without this joyful "Christmas spirit"? The poorest soul should not be forgotten at this particular time.

The children's efforts were followed by a mask ball given by the Mead Orchestra—the members of which are here constructing a telephone line. This was hugely enjoyed by all of the large number of people in attendance. A few of the old-timers opened the ball with an old-time number, which we would like to describe, but time forbids.

A prize of a very pretty bronze clock was given to the person appearing in the prettiest costume. The winner was Mrs. Orral Louquet, who appeared in a beautiful effusion that easily eclipsed all aspirants.

She represented "Innocence" and "Christmas." Her costume was made of white muslin draped with tinsel, with a "mushroom" hat to match, and a white domino. During the evening, Mr. Mead presented each gentleman with a souvenir watch fob and each lady with a souvenir hat-pin.

Deer Lodge Silver State Post, December 28, 1910

Christmas in the Plentywood Church, 1910

One of the indications that a homestead town had developed some promise of longevity was the construction of community churches and the celebration of holidays in those churches. Such was the case in Plentywood in 1910, at the new Congregational Church.

A Christmas tree and program was given last Saturday evening in the new Congregational Church in Plentywood. Although the night was stormy, a large crowd was present. The program began promptly at 8 o'clock. Mrs. Huff favored us with a beautiful instrumental solo, followed by a prayer by the Reverend Foote. This was followed by the reading of recitations and dialogues, and by the singing of songs by the school children. The selections were all well rendered and showed careful preparation.

In the midst of the program, the props of the floor of the new church gave away, owing to the heavy weight. For a few minutes it seemed as if a panic would ensue. Luckily the flooring held, and the church was quickly vacated.

Plentywood Herald, December 30, 1910

Christmas Day on the Telephone, 1911

During the twentieth century, Christmas Day developed into the heaviest long-distance use day for the nation's telephone companies. The long-distance call became the most popular means by which family members and friends bridged holiday separations. We tend to forget how long this convenience has been a part of our lives—and how successfully telephone companies have marketed the Christmas call.

*P*ROBABLY the most popular, as well as the most beneficial, innovation ever made by any great corporation in this country is that announced by the Mountain State Telephone and Telegraph Company. Herein their thousands of miles of toll lines are thrown open, at half rates, to the general public on Christmas Day. This company, whose lines traverse one-fifth of the United States, and reach into the cities, towns, camps, and ranches of Colorado, Montana, Utah, Wyoming, Idaho, and New Mexico—is certainly doing its part toward making it, indeed, a "Merry Christmas."

Since the merger of the various telephone companies, bringing into one great family all of the Midwest states, the management has been doing many

Neil Phillipps and a full coal wagon, Havre, 1912. Al Lucke Collection, Montana Historical Society Photograph Archives, Helena

things that go to prove they have the best interests of their patrons at heart. And so, on Christmas Day, from 8 o'clock in the morning until noon, the public is invited to use the toll lines freely in talking to the "dear ones at home," or whispering a "Merry Christmas" into the ear of some friend far away.

And, next to the joy to come from such a unique and unusual yuletide greeting, is the fact that this company will stand one-half the cost, bringing it within the easy reach of thousands of people who, perhaps, otherwise would not take this means of transmitting a good-cheer blessing.

In another part of this paper is the reproduction of a scene, as pictured by the artist—in which a grown son, grandchild, and grandmother are having a little talk over the long distance. It will be interesting to know how many thousands of calls will be made on Christmas morning because of the reduction in charges by the telephone company.

Deer Lodge Silver State Post, December 20, 1911

Christmas Celebration at Plains, 1914

The town of Plains's innovative 1914 plan for a community Christmas celebration would ultimately replace the Christmas-tree festivities held by individual churches while keeping the Christmas focus on children.

*A*RRANGEMENTS ARE being perfected for a Christmas Eve celebration the like of which Plains has never seen before.

Through the generosity and public spiritedness of Pete Carter, all the children in Plains and throughout the valley, under the age of 15 years, may be admitted free into the Theatorium at 7:30 p.m., on Thursday, December 24 (Christmas Eve) for this unique Christmas entertainment.

Nine reels of moving pictures will be shown, appropriate to the season, and they will appeal especially to the children.

Besides the pictures, there will be a program consisting of music and other features prepared and given by the children of the public school and the various Sunday Schools of the town.

There will be a Christmas tree and holiday decorations, and it is expected that the Honorable Santa Claus will make his appearance at this time in order to bestow a gift to every person present of the age of 15 years and under.

Committees representing every Sunday School and church in Plains are working together with Mr. Carter in this matter, and the idea of the "Municipal Christmas Tree" has the unanimous approval of all, who are co-operating to make this first affair of its kind in Plains a tremendous success.

Remember that everybody in the Plains valley is cordially invited to be present and that it will be free to all of 15 years and under. The regular admission of 25 cents will be charged at the door to persons over 15 years of age, to assist in defraying the expenses of the entertainment. Everyone come out and make this one a success!

Plains Plainsman, December 18, 1914

Christmas Editorial, Plains, 1915

The Christmas of 1915 was the second one Americans celebrated somewhat tentatively, given the raging conflict in Europe. Guy Stratton, the editor of the weekly *Plains Plainsman*, obviously felt the impact of European warfare on his readers' attitudes about the holidays. As a result, his Christmas editorial counsels rationalism in the face of impending disorder.

THANKSGIVING has passed and the Christmas holidays are upon us. Christmas is still a "Merry Christmas" for us, although the men fighting in the trenches in Europe must be able to look backward to many another Christmas which was merrier for them—and, we may hope, to look forward to other merry Christmases to come. There is just one thing that will go to make our own Christmas a more merry one, and that is, for the time being, to forget ourselves and become a "regular guy."

A regular guy is an open-hearted, open-handed, decent sort of a fellow who believes that others have a right to some happiness on earth and is willing to do his share to help them get it. It does not cost much to be a regular guy, because what we do does not decide our status so much as the spirit with which we do it.

Suppose you are so poor that you cannot afford to give even a penny away. You can smile, can't you? You can hesitate by the beggar in the street and wish him a "Merry Christmas!" You can feel in your heart that this is a season of good will to men, and show it in your bearing toward your fellow men. If the world has been good to you, now is the time to repay your debt. Give something to someone who needs it. You do not have to give much, but, if necessary, make a sacrifice.

Do not let Christmas go by without becoming human, if only for a minute. A nickel here, a dime there, a rag doll for a little girl who never had a doll, or an overcoat for the little fellow in the town who does odd jobs, who does not have an overcoat. It won't mean much to you, but it will make the Christmas merry for someone else. Loosen up! This is Christmas! Be a regular guy.

Plains Plainsman, December 19, 1915

Dillon's Municipal Celebration, 1916

The war in Europe had commenced in 1914, but the United States did not enter World War I until April of 1917. By the Christmas of 1916, however, few Americans could ignore the ominous implications of the European struggle. During that holiday season, particular emphasis fell on the refugees of the European conflict—and that emphasis shaped the community Christmas celebrations in such towns as Dillon.

*T*HE MUNICIPAL CHRISTMAS celebration held on the night of Christmas was well attended, the auditorium of the City Hall being crowded almost to its capacity. The stage was decorated appropriately for the occasion. The exercises opened with music by the orchestra, followed by the singing of "It Came Upon a Midnight Clear" by the audience. The story of the birth of Christ was read from Luke's gospel by Dr. Robert Clark.

The pageant depicted the plight of the children in the war-stricken regions of Europe and began with the entering of the Spirit of Christmas— the part being played by Mrs. Tom Luebben—who was accompanied by the Snow Fairy. The Spirit of Christmas told why we love to give at Christmas. The children representing little folks starving in Armenia, Belgium, Romania, and Poland then entered and, after telling of their pitiful plight, asked for food and clothing from the children of America.

Mrs. R. R. Rathbone, as America, appealed to the children of Dillon, who answered the request and passed through the audience, taking up a generous offering. They placed this collection at the feet of the Spirit of Christmas, who gave it to America. Miss Zetta Gilbert, as the Red Cross Nurse, then entered and took charge of the offering, stating that the money would be spent in the manner designated by the contributors.

All joined in the singing of "America," which was followed by a clever rendition of a violin solo by Miss Helen Finch.

The entire audience joined in singing "Hark, the Herald Angels Sing" and "Silent Night," which closed the exercises.

Yesterday the committee in charge of the celebration counted the contributions and it was found that a total of $411 was received, the Odd Fellows lodge giving $100 of that amount. Of this money, $250 will go to the Armenians, $30 to the Polish, and $50 to the Belgians. The rest will be distributed by the American Red Cross Society.

Dillon Examiner, December 27, 1916

Entertainment at Glendale, 1916

In the 1880s, the mining town of Glendale in Beaverhead County boasted almost 3,000 residents—but that population had fallen to less than 100 by 1916. Nevertheless, Christmas celebrations remained a central bonding aspect of winter life.

THE OLD CHURCH at Glendale was once more crowded to its limit with Melrose people by an entertainment given by the Glendale School and their teacher, Miss Ahern. Although seven pupils gave one of the best two-hour entertainments that could be expected, Miss Ahern certainly deserves a great deal of credit, as her scholars were trained to perfection. Seven 4-horse loads and 4 automobiles attended from Melrose.

The Melrose Military Band attended in full force and gave five of their choice selections. Otto Boetticher was sure that each selection required a drum part.

Dillon Examiner, December 27, 1916

The Annual Return of Young Adults, 1916

After the turn of the century, as new technologies, a homesteading boom, and vagaries of the West's economy made Montana's society more complex, an interesting Christmas phenomenon developed: the annual return of a community's youth who had left to pursue jobs or education. This reunion of families for the holidays is noted particularly in Dillon, just prior to World War I.

*M*ANY OF THE Dillon young folks who are teaching school in other parts of the state, or who are attending college away from here, are home to spend the holidays with relatives.

This group of bobsledders paused to be photographed in front of the Eureka Public Library circa 1908. Montana Historical Society Photograph Archives, Helena

Misses Josephine Erwin and Elizabeth Sutherland arrived Saturday evening from Lewistown, where they are employed in the city school. Miss Sutherland will not return to Lewistown, but on January 1 will assume her duties as Superintendent of Schools of Beaverhead County, having been elected to that position last November.

Miss Margaret Poindexter, musical instructor in a prominent young ladies' seminary at Sycamore, Illinois, is here for two weeks, and Miss Jessie Poindexter, teacher in the Harlowton High School, is spending the mid-winter vacation with her mother and sisters at this place.

Miss Ethel Adams, who is teaching in a consolidated school district in the Flathead country, is spending Christmas week at home from Ronan.

Miss Montana Gilbert, who is teaching in the same district at Dixon, is also here for two weeks.

Misses May Smith, Marian Leach, Helen Finch, and Lucille Paul, Dillon girls attending the state university, are here from Missoula to enjoy the holiday season at their homes.

Lawrence Price, Fred Finch, Phil Guidici, and Charles Carroll arrived Saturday from Bozeman, where they are attending the state agricultural college.

Dillon Examiner, December 27, 1916

Christmas in Wolf Point, 1918

With the end of World War I (November 11, 1918), the country had little time to return to normalcy prior to Christmas. However, the pride of victory and the release from some wartime rationing constraints generated a euphoria that reached into the smallest of Montana communities.

*F*ROM A BUSINESS point of view, Christmas, 1918, will go into the records as the best ever. "Great! Much better than anticipated!" was the substance of the answer received in every place where inquiry was made, which included nearly all the stores in town. By the evening of the 24th, the stores, which had offered splendid stocks, showed shelves and showcases nearly empty. The trade demonstrated that it had far greater buying power than was supposed. Purchases were liberal and cash was the rule.

The post office had visible proof of the volume of local holiday business. The number of packages was at least twice as great as were ever handled before. The night of the 21st alone, 38 sacks of parcels were hauled to the trains. There was nearly as much the following Monday night. The incoming mail was also extremely heavy.

Well-prepared exercises, with beautifully decorated trees and pleasing programs, were held Christmas Eve at the Methodist Episcopal and Presbyterian Churches. Collections were taken at both churches for the suffering Armenians. After brief appeals had been made by the pastors, the Reverend Nelson and the Reverend McInor, a total of $25.00 was realized.

The weather both before and after Christmas has been close to perfect—clear, crisp, and calm—lacking only snow to make it ideal. But few, excepting boys and girls with visions of new sleds, found any fault with the absence of more than a trace of the beautiful.

Altogether it was a glorious Christmastide, with the spirit of peace and good will resting over the community.

Wolf Point Herald, December 26, 1918

Christmas and the Spanish Influenza Epidemic in Columbia Falls, 1918

In 1918 Montana sent thousands of its young men to World War I and suffered devastating drought on its high plains. In addition, an epidemic of Spanish influenza swept the state, causing the deaths of hundreds on the home front. By Christmas of 1918, the worst of the epidemic had run its course, and county and municipal health officers had begun to reduce restrictions on public gatherings.

THE INFLUENZA BAN in Columbia Falls is lifted, word to that effect having been issued yesterday by Dr. John T. Robinson and the City Health Board.

A Merry Christmas and a Happy New Year

COLUMBIA FALLS, MONTANA

GREETINGS FROM COLUMBIA FALLS

The inset photograph of Columbia Falls localizes this Christmas greeting. Montana Historical Society Photograph Archives, Helena

Church services will be permitted and the local moving-picture house will be allowed to operate. School, however, will not commence until the first of the year.

Instead of the old plan of quarantining the public and allowing the patients their freedom, a strict quarantine will be placed upon all persons having the disease and they will be isolated, the same as diphtheria or scarlet-fever cases. Any violation will be prosecuted according to the city ordinances.

It is believed by the Health Board that this plan will keep the disease in check and, at the same time, permit the resumption of business and social activities.

The old order affecting saloons and pool halls is still in force, and the holding dances will not be permitted as yet.

With the quarantine being raised, the members of the Montana Soldiers Home will be able to get out in time to do their usual Christmas shopping. Several veterans who have been held out of the Home on account of the "Flu Ban" will also be allowed to enroll.

Columbia Falls Columbian, December 19, 1918

Billy Gemmell and the Joshers' Club in Butte, 1916

The creation of the Joshers' Club in Al Green's saloon just before Christmas 1904 began one of Butte's more inspiring stories of private-sector charity work among the city's needy. Literally thousands of Butte families benefitted from the work of Billy Gemmell and his associates, whose work only ended when the federal government assumed responsibility for relief in 1933. Gemmell had worked as a railroad agent and a coal supplier prior to becoming a Silver Bow County commissioner. He died tragically in a 1927 fire.

*T*WELVE YEARS AGO, about this time of the year or perhaps a little earlier, there gathered in a Butte saloon a bunch of good fellows. They had heard of a number of needy people, without food, clothing, or fuel in the city. It was a cold night, and the advance notices issued by the weather man were not encouraging. Possessed of the Christmas spirit, they looked over the list of the needy that had been reported and saw to it that the handful of families were well provided with the necessities of life—and the provisions furnished that year were sufficient to last a long time.

To cut a long story short, it was out of this one little gathering that there has grown up in Butte an "organization" without officers and without charter, which has made it its business to see that no one in the great copper camp is without food and sustenance during the Christmas season. In the past 12 years, it has given aid and succor to thousands.

The name of this organization is the "Joshers' Club." The name is not appropriate, however, because its work is serious and sincere. Some of the newspaper boys hung the name to it and the name stuck. But the "club," if it can be so called, is no "josh."

Those who are active in the handling of this annual charity are unselfish. Names of donors are never mentioned, except in outstanding instances. The men who give their time and money generously are never listed in the press, but their names must surely be written down in the big book above, among those who love their fellow men.

There is one, however, whose name is featured every year as the moving spirit of the Joshers' Club. He is known as plain "Billy" Gemmell.

Gemmell has done the hard work. He has kept the Joshers alive. He purchases the immense quantity of foodstuffs annually delivered to the needy and has, through his wonderful personality, made possible all that has been accomplished by the organization.

One has to know Gemmell to appreciate him.

Billy Gemmell is a most unique character. He made a success and a moderate fortune out of the racing game. There is no man in Montana of consequence who does not call him by his first name. He is a bon vivant and a good fellow who has lived his own life and never bothered with the ideas of anyone else. And he has seen to it that many of the unfortunate have not suffered from a lack of the milk of human kindness. He has been the soul of the Joshers' Club, and when he passes the organization will pass also. His dynamic energy crystalizes in this annual effort, and it is doubtful if another man could be found in Butte to take up his work and carry it to a successful conclusion.

The history of the Joshers may be briefly told: The organization cares for hundreds of families every holiday season. Even with great prosperity, such as Butte usually enjoys, there is much abject poverty. Wives lose husbands, sickness prevents employment, and a thousand things help to swell the multitude of the needy. The Joshers this year will provide not only Christmas cheer for one day, but provisions, clothing, and other necessities of life sufficient to last for a couple of weeks. Every family in need is amply provided for.

This year the Joshers are in greater need than ever. While the support financially will be as great as before, it must be remembered that the prices of provisions and meat are literally sky high. This means that more strenuous efforts must be made to "deliver the goods." This is why Billy Gemmell is the busiest charity worker in Montana this year.

This is the story of Billy Gemmell, bon vivant, and his Joshers' Club. It is a real charity, the kind that warms the cockles of the heart. It has grown into an institution, and the warm-hearted people of the great mining town are proud of it, and of the man who made it.

Montana Newspaper Association Insert series, December 21, 1916

Christmas at the Twin Bridges Orphanage, 1921

Christmas always has proved an important holiday for the residents of Montana's state institutions, including the Soldiers' Home in Columbia Falls, the School for the Deaf and Blind at Boulder, and the Tuberculosis Hospital at Galen. In particular, though, Christmas festivities were eagerly anticipated by the children at the Twin Bridges Orphans' Home, which operated from 1894 to 1975 and cared for more than 5,000 children.

*C*HILDREN IN THE State Orphans' Home at Twin Bridges will have as happy a Christmas as the average child on the outside. As nearly as possible, the Yuletide will be observed just as it would be in any private home, and Santa Claus will not neglect those unfortunate in having lost their mothers and fathers.

For a number of the 225 children in the home, gifts will be received from relatives and friends. But the majority will be provided for in other ways, principally through the generosity of officers of the institution and of other organizations charitably engaged in the dispensation of Christmas cheer.

For each child, in consequence, there will be one or more presents, delivered by old St. Nick himself, appropriately attired in regulation costume. In turn, he will call at each of the 12 cottages, presenting his gifts and wishing each child a brimming cup of Yuletide cheer and happiness.

In each cottage also will stand a Christmas tree suitably decorated for the occasion. This evening a Christmas entertainment will be given, and on Christmas Day the children will enjoy a dinner that will be unsurpassed anywhere.

Preparations for a befitting Christmas were begun two weeks ago by Mr. and Mrs. H. W. George, president and matron respectively, of the State Orphans' Home. A special trip was made to Butte to purchase Christmas gifts and a goodly supply of candies, nuts, popcorn, and oranges. The later will be placed in colored mosquito-bar bags, one of which will be given to each child. Tree decorations were also secured, and an order was placed for the dozen firs which will be required by the Home.

While several organizations have promised voluntarily to remember a number of the children with Christmas gifts, the Butte Boy Scouts have made special preparations to that end in repairing and rebuilding used toys they have collected. In addition to other gifts they receive, each child is therefore likely to be made a present of at least one of these toys from the Scout Organization.

The Christmas entertainment, which is to be given this evening in the auditorium of the Home by the children (under the direction of the matron and teachers) includes songs, recitations, and drills.

Few persons will dine more sumptuously on Christmas Day than the children in the Home, who will partake of a dinner consisting of roast goose with dressing, mashed potatoes, candied sweet potatoes, mixed sweet potatoes, cranberry sauce, brown gravy, green peas, celery, fruit salad with whipped cream, mincemeat pie and cheese, bread and butter, and milk.

Provided the weather is cold enough, the older children will go skating in the afternoon, while others will enjoy the toys they have received.

Anaconda Standard, December 22, 1921

Anode Poetry

The Anaconda Copper Mining Company (at the behest of its workers' many labor unions) emphasized safety on the job through a number of campaigns and publicity mechanisms. For years it published a monthly safety magazine, *The Anode*, that urged Company employees to practice safe work habits. In *The Anode*'s December edition for 1922, a clever writer combined Charles Dickens's "A Christmas Carol" with Clement C. Moore's "A Visit from St. Nicholas" to render an elaborate safety message.

The Curse of a Wandering Mind

'Twas the night before Xmas, I woke with a start,
My "innards" were churning, head splitting apart,
One arm in a sling and a cast on the other,
My ribs pressed my lungs till I thought I would smother,
In the palms of my hands was a burning sensation,
Through the soles of my feet pins and needles kept chasin',
My legs were in splints and then bandaged together,

The top of my head felt as light as a feather,
"Good gracious alive!" I heard myself say,
"What a h—l of a fix to be Xmas day!"

The moon shining palely outside on the snow,
Peeped in through the sash with a timorous glow,
When into this dimly illumined reflection
Bounced old Santa Claus, with a queer genuflection.
"Ha, Ha!" cried the Saint, "'Tis a thing of the past
Putting luck before judgment! Your luck cannot last.
'Twould be justice to leave you! Your bruises and pains.
An example for others with functionless brains."
"Don't leave me! Please help me!" cried I in dismay,
"Just think of my laddie and his Xmas day."

"Try thinking yourself; and keep thinking of others,
Of grief brought to sweethearts, of tears brought to mothers;
Just think of the children who now need a daddy
To round out their Xmas, like your little laddie;
Then, think of the chances you take underground,
While 'Devil-May-Care' throws his shadow around,
And chuckles with glee at a dangerous condition
He hopes may send you and your Pard to perdition."
"Have mercy, Old Timer! This day in December
The welfare of others I'll swear to remember!"

Santa smiled through the whiskers that covered his features,
"You miners are tough. You need strenuous teachers;
So I gave you a cut and a bruise for the men
Your carelessness hurt in the Con, and the Penn.
These fractures and breaks, I threw in for the two
Poor 'green-horn' Bohunks you maimed in the View.
And that cut in hour head which first caused you to faint,
Is a 'ringer' for one you gave Jim, in the Saint."

"Don't go any further!" I cried in despair,
"After this, I'll work only with caution and care."

"To drive home this lesson, I've had to deceive,
I've put you in torture to make you believe
That ninety per cent of all accidents happen
To men who are caught with their faculties nappin'!
Therefore," said Santa, "My gifts will be few;
Because of the thousands distributed to,
Peruse well this pamphlet—the first of its kind
Entitled: 'The Curse of a Wandering Mind.' "
To the crashing of sleigh bells, I woke with a shock!
My lad had the bells I had placed in his sock.

W. F. C., "The Curse of a Wandering Mind,"
The Anode, December 1922

The Delayed Christmas, Valley County, 1924

In 1959 Mrs. Frances Barton entered her account of a homesteader's Christmas on Crow Creek in the *Glasgow Courier*'s "Christmas Memory Contest." She won the competition with her reminiscence of her family's postponed Christmas of 1924. The Bartons' homestead was located about 35 miles north of Hinsdale, near the Valley County–Phillips County line.

$\mathcal{C}$HRISTMAS, 1924, found us living in a two-room, sod-roofed, tar-paper covered homestead shack on Crow Creek, in northern Valley County, only a few miles from the Canadian line. Since early in December we had been isolated by successive snowstorms, raging blizzards, and excessively cold weather. These had prevented us from making the 14-mile trip to the little crossroads' post office and general-merchandise store established in 1916 and known as Genevieve.

Our chief anxiety had been that some accident or illness would befall our six-month-old son, John. But he had remained his usual healthy, happy self and couldn't have cared less that no bright Christmas packages, cards or mail

Waiting for a Chinook, by Charles M. Russell (watercolor, 1886). On loan from Montana Stockgrowers' Association, Montana Historical Society Museum, Helena

had been sent or received—or that his parents, in their spare time were reading back numbers of *Hunter-Trader-Trapper*, *Successful Farming*, and the *Saturday Evening Post*, carefully stored for three years past on a high shelf in the bedroom.

Each day we had hoped that the weather would moderate enough to permit a trip with team and jumper to Genevieve, but Christmas Day dawned to find us still having to make do with just what we had on hand. We wished each other a "Merry Christmas" and sang carols contained in our Methodist hymnal, accompanied by me on the little old organ we had purchased at a farm sale just that fall. I prepared a meal as festive as our supplies allowed. But, when these things were done, that was it—the third Christmas on that ranch and a very dull one indeed.

The cold, stormy weather continued until around the 10th day of the new year of 1925. Then there came what the oldtimers call a "January thaw." On a fine, sunny day, my husband successfully made the trip to Genevieve and—with the accumulated mail of a month, containing cards, letters, gifts, magazines, and local papers, together with fresh supplies—Christmas finally came to the Barton family. And once again we felt in touch with the outside world.

Glasgow Courier, December 20, 1984

Railroad Greetings, 1924

The Publicity Department of the Great Northern Railway Company never was accused of missing an opportunity to capitalize on an occasion that might reflect sympathetically on the railroad. The Great Northern engaged in just this type of corporate-Christmas commemoration in 1924.

*T*HE GREAT NORTHERN RAILWAY distributed a rather novel Christmas "Greeting" on its one hundred or more passenger trains that were traveling east and west between Chicago and the Pacific Northwest cities on Christmas Day. Simultaneously this "Greeting" was handed out upon steamships crossing the Pacific, between Asiatic ports and Seattle.

Every passenger received a copy of this artistically illustrated booklet, entitled "The Oriental and Captain Palmer." It tells the story of transportation progress made in the Oriental trade mediums from the period of the slow sailing vessel to the present-day fast steamship (and its great aiding complement, the steam railway) which have cut the old world-new world voyages from months to days. Captain Nathaniel Brown Palmer devised the fastest ships to go around the American continent, but it remained for James J. Hill

Snowbound on the Jaw Bone, the Montana Railroad, later part of the Milwaukee Road, circa 1899. Holmboe and White, photographers, Montana Historical Society Photograph Archives, Helena

to build the shortest route across it. Besides, a copy of the booklet was given to each of the thirty thousand or more employees of the Great Northern Railway from the section man to the vice-president. Copies also were sent to all ticket agents of foreign railway lines throughout the United States.

Conrad Independent-Observer, January 1, 1925

C. E. Aspling's Christmas Editorial, Deer Lodge, 1925

The economic depression that undermined Montana's development during the 1920s proved a harsh disappointment after the promise anticipated by the victors in World War I. In his annual Christmas editorial, C. E. Aspling, the publisher of the *Silver State Post* in Deer Lodge, addresses this disappointment in the context of the spirit of Christmases past and present.

$\mathcal{A}$RTHUR GUY EMPEY, famous for the story he wrote about the Great War, "Over the Top," tells about a Christmas he experienced in the trenches. As the day approached, the fervor of the fighting slackened. Everybody was thinking of home and loved ones, and there wasn't much joy in the business of killing.

By Christmas Eve, the firing had practically ceased. The men lay in their muddy trench, pictures of happier Christmas Eves, before the world had become a slaughterhouse, coming into their minds. Just a little way across the patch of gloom in front of them were the German trenches. "Fritz," too, was thinking of other Christmas Eves, when he trimmed the trees for his little brothers and sisters, or his own boys and girls, instead of killing somebody he didn't know and had no personal grudge against, in the trench across the way.

Suddenly from the German trench there came the sound of cornet playing "There's a Long, Long Trail A-Winding." That was a favorite song of the British Tommies, with whom Empey (an American who enlisted before we entered the war) was serving as a machine gunner. The Germans must have

Decorators used mechanical assistance to adorn the tree in front of the Butte Courthouse circa 1917. Montana Historical Society Photograph Archives, Helena

heard the British soldiers singing it often. Soon, from the British trenches, arose a sweet and powerful voice singing the words of the song to the accompaniment of the German cornet.

And so, in the midst of the war, with all its cruelty and hatred, for a little while there was that "Peace on Earth, Good Will to Men" of which the herald angels sang on that glad night of long ago.

The Great War has ended these many years, but the world has not yet reached that state of Christian civilization where hatred and cruelty no longer find lodgment in the hearts of men. It never will reach that blessed state until the teachings of Him whose natal day we celebrate are so engraved on human hearts that there is no room left in them for evil.

But—just as the British and Germans stopped fighting at Christmas to join each other in a song that suggested home and loved ones—so, in the bitterness, the misunderstanding, and the unkindness of human relationships, we pause at Christmas to forget our spites, our jealousies, and our hatreds. And we join with those whom we ordinarily choose to regard with an unfriendly eye in an armistice of peace and good will.

This annual observance of Christmas is a good thing for all of us. But how much better it would be if we could make the spirit of Christmas last throughout the year. What a kinder, happier world we would have if Jesus' admonition to love thy neighbor as thyself were held in more respect. Admittedly, we cannot achieve this goal—we can only try. But do we really try?

This business of circulating hideous lies to arouse and perpetuate hatred, unfortunately, is not a purely wartime function. In His name, we should call a truce on all manner of such evil at Christmas and, even though we cannot love our neighbors as ourselves, we can try to treat them with courtesy and kindliness.

Why cannot we carry this manifestation of the Christmas spirit, which is the Christmas spirit, through the whole year that is to follow—making 1926 a far better, happier, and holier year than was 1925?

Deer Lodge Silver State Post, December 24, 1925

Deer Lodge Community Christmas, 1925

In many Montana towns of modest population size, the general practice of church-based Christmas-tree celebrations overlapped with community-tree festivities during the 1920s. Such was the case in Deer Lodge in 1925 where a family could choose among several Christmas activities, or attend them all.

*W*ITH THE PROGRAM of the Deer Lodge community Christmas tree scheduled to open at 7:30 o'clock this evening and programs of various churches given during the week, residents of this section have had more than Christmas shopping to occupy their attention. To-night will be the big night. Mothers and dads are requested to bring their children to the tree in time for the opening number. Later they will witness the antics of Santa Claus, who will arrive upon the scene in great style. After the singing of Christmas carols by the members of the Deer Lodge Male Chorus and a chorus composed of ladies, the gifts from the tree will be distributed by St. Nicholas.

Christmas programs for the youngsters were carried out in great style Wednesday evening by the Sunday Schools of the Presbyterian Church, the Christian Church, the Episcopal Church, and the Methodist Church. The programs were very complete with songs, recitations by the children, and the tendering of gifts by Santa Claus. On Christmas night the management of the Hotel Deer Lodge will entertain the Deer Lodge folks at the hotel in the two banquet rooms.

Deer Lodge Silver State Post, December 24, 1925

Christmas Turkey Trade, 1925

Tens of thousands of homesteaders left Montana during the agricultural "bust" of the late 1910s and early 1920s. Those farmers and stockmen who hunkered down and survived had adapted their operations to the weather, to the land, and to the demands of the market. During the 1920s, many Montana farmers became gobbler gauchos because the Thanksgiving and Christmas markets for these birds in the East proved quite profitable.

*W*ITH THE TURKEY marketing season virtually ended, figures obtained at the Great Falls railroad offices show growers in north-central Montana this year received $500,000 for their crop. Records at the offices of the Milwaukee Road disclose that 43 carloads of turkeys have been shipped out of the territory this fall.

The estimate of returns to growers is based on minimum car loadings of 30,000 pounds to the car. Many of the cars were loaded heavier than that. The price is figured at 38 cents a pound, whereas the price now is 40 cents, and many shipments are bringing 39 cents. The Thanksgiving market paid 34 to 36 cents a pound, but only a small part of the crop was marketed then.

Carload shipments from the following points are shown by railroads in Great Falls:

Havre, 10; Great Falls, 9; Lewistown, 8; Conrad, 5; Choteau, 2; one each from Sweet Grass, Judith Gap, Augusta, Geyser, Moccasin, Valier, Brady, Chinook, Denton, Geraldine, and Danvers.

If none of the cars exceeded the minimum loading weight of 30,000 pounds, the 43 cars of turkeys at 38 cents a pound brought $480,000. A car shipped from Valier this week brought $11,000. A car from Lewistown contained 3,500 birds. If each bird weighed only 10 pounds, this meant $13,650 for the car, at 39 cents a pound.

That 10 pounds was not the average weight is seen from the report that the weight went as high as 32 pounds. One farmer at Great Falls received $67 for 13 birds, or a fraction more than $5 a turkey. If he was paid only 38 cents a pound, his birds averaged more than 13 pounds in weight.

Most of the birds for the Christmas trade are going to the Atlantic Seaboard—New York and Boston taking some of them. Although freight shipments are virtually all gone, there is still a possibility that some birds will go out by express, as was the case just before Thanksgiving, when the American Express Company here sent two carloads to Seattle.

The turkey output at places other than here listed is not considered, as the information is not available. It is known that Livingston and Bozeman are among the cities which have shipped turkeys this year, at least one carload from each point. Great Northern points east of Chinook have made turkey shipments this season also, it is reported at railroad offices in Great Falls.

Conrad Independent Observer, December 17, 1925

Anaconda Salvation Army, 1925

The economic depression that hit Montana's agricultural regions during the 1920s also extended into its urban centers. In smaller communities, religious groups worked to alleviate the problems of the needy. But, in more populous towns, several service organizations assumed those responsibilities during the holidays. In the smelter city of Anaconda, such a group was the Salvation Army.

 $\mathcal{P}$ ROVIDING ANACONDANS keep the Salvation Army kettles at the boiling point during the short time left before Christmas, every needy family in the city will enjoy a delicious dinner on the best of all holidays, according to Captain Robert Hodge, who is in charge of the work in Anaconda. The return from the kettles placed on Anaconda streets is very slow so far, he states, but it is expected that enough funds will be secured to furnish a Christmas basket of goodies to all of the needy families.

The Christmas season is the Salvation Army's busiest time, and its members make special efforts at this time to furnish the comforts and cheer to unfortunate persons and families who otherwise would be unable to enjoy the holiday. Each case that comes to the notice of the members of the Army is thoroughly investigated before the aid is given, and it has been found in Anaconda that there are several cases that need help immediately.

Do you know that in Anaconda there are families who often go a whole day without a meal, and that a number of children are not given the food that is essential to their growth and development? According to Captain Hodge, there are many such cases reported each week—in fact every day—and at present many are being called to the attention of the Salvation Army. As an example, a few days ago a case was discovered of a sick woman living in Anaconda, whose nine small children are suffering for want of proper food and attention. As soon as the case was reported, supplies were given them out of the Army pantry (the stores being closed) to tide the unfortunate family over until the next day.

It is to help such cases as these that the kettles are placed on Anaconda streets each Christmas. Here persons passing by may drop in a small bit of change to help in the bringing of Christmas cheer to unfortunate families in the city.

Preparations are being made by the Salvation Army here to serve the Christmas baskets (containing everything essential to a genuine Christmas dinner) to the needy, and with each basket will go a copy of the Christmas number of the *War Cry*. The Army has received 1,000 copies of this special number, which will be placed on sale this coming week. It contains a number of articles written upon subjects pertinent to the season, and a beautiful cover design in holiday colors gives this issue a gay appearance. Copies of the *War Cry* will also be distributed at the state penitentiary at Deer Lodge and at the state hospital at Warm Springs.

On Christmas Eve a big Christmas tree, gaily decorated, will form the center of the stage for the Christmas program which will be held at the Salvation Army Hall for the children of the city. Dialogues, readings, and Christmas songs will be included in the program, which will be followed by the distribution of presents to the children by old Santa Claus himself. No child will be overlooked by Santa when he delivers his presents.

After the exercises at the Salvation Army Hall, the lassies will distribute the Christmas baskets to the needy in the city, so that they can start early Christmas morning to prepare the dinner. Anacondans who wish to contribute to the "Christmas Cheer Fund" of the Army may send or bring their contributions of food, money, or clothing to the Army Hall, where they will be greatly appreciated, according to Captain Hodge.

Anaconda Standard, December 13, 1925

Letters to Santa Claus from Columbia Falls, 1926

The Yuletide tradition of a child writing his letter to Santa Claus began in earnest during the Victorian era and gathered momentum after World War I. Occasionally the crafty grade-school teacher would turn this practice into a writing assignment during a time when students otherwise showed little dedication to school work. And some of these pieces found their way into the local newspapers—as was the case in Columbia Falls in 1926.

THE FOLLOWING LETTERS were sent to Santa Claus, Icy Cape, Alaska, in care of this newspaper, and dated December 14, 1926:

DEAR SANTA CLAUS: I will thank you for all you have brought us in the past. Will you please bring me a tool chest and a sled too?
—With love to you, James Marantette

DEAR SANTA CLAUS: Are you coming with your reindeer this year? If you do, will you please bring me something? I don't want much. I do want a new doll because my doll's arm is off. I want a wrist watch. If you will, you might as well bring me some candy too. That isn't all I want; I want alot more. I want some paints. Oh, hold your horses. I want more. I want a new dress because mine is torn. That's about all I want.
—With love, Evelyn Saurey

The Orr children of Dillon hung their stockings and waited for Santa, circa 1928. Montana Historical Society Photograph Archives, Helena

DEAR SANTA CLAUS: Will you please bring me a book, a game, and a stocking of candy? If you will bring me these things, I will try to be a good girl. I will not throw snow balls at you this year.

Well, Santa, I will tell you why I want these things. I should like to have a book to read. I have read all the books I have, over and over until I almost know them by heart. I want a game because I have none. I want some candy and nuts because I like them very much.

Santa, please be sure not to forget my little brother in Spokane and bring enough to make him as happy as possible. I will write you some other time and tell you what my other brothers want.

—Your loving little friend, Julia Luce

Columbia Falls Forum, December 23, 1926

The "Xmas" Issue, 1926

Although Americans tend to think that controversies surrounding the Christmas holidays are relatively recent in development, that infrequently is the case. The argument over of the use of "Xmas" is a case in point. That issue was addressed by the editor of the Deer Lodge weekly in 1926.

*T*HERE ALWAYS MAY be found a lot of good gentlemen who are ready to seize the opportunity to magnify a triviality into a great moral issue. Some of them have just discovered that a mortal sin is being committed by writing it "Xmas," instead of spelling it out as "Christmas."

According to a New York dispatch, a campaign has been started to ban the long-used abbreviation, which is declared to be irreverent, with a "subtle tendency to destroy the beautiful thoughts in connection with Christmas." This will perhaps be news to many who have occasionally written "Xmas" with no thoughts of irreverence.

The letter X, or more properly the Greek letter Chi, which is similar in form, was used as a symbol denoting Christ from the time of Constantine, centuries before the English term was known. Webster gives "Xmas" as a good abbreviation or contraction for "Christmas"; also "Xn" for "Christian," and "Xnty" for "Christianity."

Personally, we do not care for the abbreviation "Xmas," and never write it so, but there is certainly no reason for getting excited because some one else does. The relationship of the average reformer to the jackass seldom has been more convincingly shown than in this latest "movement" to eliminate "Xmas."

Maybe they'll pass a law about it.

Deer Lodge Silver State Post, December 30, 1926

Conrad Decorates for Christmas, 1928

Conrad, the county seat of Pondera County, has served for decades as a supply center for agricultural activities in the "Golden Triangle," the vast expanse of wheat-growing country in north-central Montana. The festive decorations proved alluring to the farmers and their families who made infrequent visits to town. By the late 1920s, stores across Montana had developed the annual practice of featuring Christmas decorations.

CONRAD STORES show more beautiful holiday decorations and wonderfully decorated show windows than in any previous year. In fact, the visitor to the city is impressed with the spirit of Christmas and good will of the holiday season, by the decorations alone, if for no other reason.

Take the efforts of the Drake Drug Company, for instance. The idea of evergreen trees along the store's frontage, on both streets, is something out of the ordinary for Conrad. It makes a very pretty effect, besides having many beautiful show windows full of gift merchandise.

The electrically lighted Christmas tree on the top of the Conrad Mercantile Store is a delight to young and old, and in the evening makes a wonderful effect from the streets below. Their large show windows on each street are overflowing with Christmas cheer—a delight to the early shopper.

Manager Stuart of the Golden Rule exhibits three of the best show windows in the city and has set a new mark with his display work in these large, beautifully decorated windows, which are a delight to both young and old.

The new Buttrey Store is beautifully decorated both inside and out, and their large show windows spread holiday cheer to every shopper that visits their new department store. Their decorative effects are both novel and new in this city.

The show windows of the Riggs Mercantile Store, as well as the large, double store room itself, are holiday pictures of gifts, and good things to eat, and they extend a welcome to the Christmas shoppers.

The Pondera Drug Company's large room is a thing of beauty, and the huge space is literally overflowing with holiday goods and decoration of every description. Their large show windows are especially pretty, both during the day and at night when the lighting effects are wonderful.

Almost every place of business shows excellent taste in the Christmas and holiday decorations, all of which help to make the city a thing of beauty and joy to the out-of-town visitors as well as home folk.

Conrad Independent-Observer, December 13, 1928

Brady Christmas News, 1929

By the late 1920s, hundreds of rural, farm communities—like Brady in Pondera County—had suffered hard times since World War I, and they would suffer harder times during the 1930s. Yet, Brady's residents preserved the church-based homesteader tradition of a Christmas-tree celebration.

THE METHODIST EPISCOPAL church was filled for the Christmas entertainment Wednesday evening. The special program was one of the best ever, and the cantata by the Epworth League was splendid, as the young people taking part had been well trained. Santa Claus appeared on schedule, and everyone enjoyed a treat as well as a fine evening of genuine entertainment.

The Brady schools have but one week of vacation at Christmas time, school opening again on Monday, December 30th.

Conrad Independent-Observer, December 26, 1929

Conrad Christmas Tidbits, 1929

Residents of Pondera County who chose not to dine at home were offered delectable fare at the Conrad Hotel on the occasion of Christmas 1929. From the menu, one would not guess that the stock-market crash had occurred just weeks before and that Montana was about to slide inexorably into the Great Depression of the 1930s.

*H*EREWITH WE PUBLISH the Christmas-dinner menu which will be served at the Conrad Hotel. Ever thoughtful of their patrons—and especially those who want something a little different—they have received a special shipment of buffalo meat. This meat was shipped from near Kalispell, and the management has secured some choice cuts from a three-year-old steer. This is the first time that buffalo steaks have ever been served in Conrad. They will start serving buffalo meat on Sunday, December 22nd, and this choice viand is included in their special Christmas menu. The following is available for Christmas dinner at $1.50 per plate:

Cream of Tomato Soup

Celery   Olives

Fruit Salad

Fillet of Finnan Haddie

Buffalo Steak with Garnish

Roast Turkey, Cranberry Sauce

Oyster Dressing

Roast Goose, Apple Nut Dressing

Mashed Potatoes and Gravy

Cauliflower in Butter

Hot Parker House Rolls

Pumpkin or Mince Pie

Plum Pudding Fruit Cake

Conrad Independent-Observer, December 19, 1929

Harlowton Christmas Charity, 1932

Harlowton, Wheatland County's seat, was created as a stockmen's town, but became a railroad division point when the Milwaukee Road wove its mainline through Montana in 1906. Harlowton's residents long have demonstrated strong support for numerous civic projects. Christmas in the Depression would prove no detriment to the town's spirit.

Great Falls Firemen's Christmas toy hospital, December 13, 1923. Montana Historical Society Photograph Archives, Helena

COMMUNITY EXERCISES were held here around the big Shrine Christmas tree, and about 800 sacks of candy and nuts were distributed to children who came from all parts of Wheatland County to see Santa Claus, impersonated by John Olson of this city. The magnificent fir tree was brought from the Castle Mountains by Charles Bolin. Forty-four smaller trees were placed up and down Central Avenue by other Shriners.

About 90 families received boxes filled with food and supplies from the funds raised at the free public matinee. Admission was a donation of canned goods or Christmas delectables. Manager and Mrs. Moore sponsored this idea. Gib McFarland of Big Elk delivered a 1,200 pound beef, and many other offerings of supplies were made by generous-hearted ranchers.

The young people of the Federated Church toured the town singing Christmas carols, and a Christmas program was given in the Presbyterian Church and at the Trinity Lutheran Church. The usual midnight mass was celebrated at St. Joseph's Catholic Church, and the edifice did not have standing room. Father L. O. LeGriss, pastor, preached an eloquent sermon.

Despite the depression, there wasn't a family in Wheatland County without an ample supply for Christmas.

Lewistown Democrat-News, December 28, 1932

Stanford's Toy Hospital, 1932

Stanford is the county seat of Judith Basin County and is located on the route between Great Falls and Lewistown. One of the town's 1932 Christmas projects illustrates not only the community's agricultural base, but also how it coped with the Depression.

*T*HE ANNUAL TOY HOSPITAL and clinic sponsored by the members of the Judith Basin chapter of the Future Farmers of America, is bringing to a close another successful program.

Broken toys have been collected around the community, repaired and remodeled, painted with Christmas colors, and placed with other toys that have been made in farm shops from scrap lumber saved during the year.

Last year more than 40 children received several toys each from this source. This year the list contains more than 60 names. The members of the organization will deliver the toys to the families on Christmas morning in true Christmas style, with sled and jingling bells.

Lewistown Democrat-News, December 28, 1932

Butte Serbian Christmas, 1934

In many Montana communities, ethnic holiday traditions survived for decades —and some survive to this day. The mining city of Butte was especially rich in ethnic-neighborhood festivities, as this description of a traditional Serbian celebration of Christmas attests.

*C*HRISTMAS CAME to a little colony of people in Butte and their friends in south-western Montana at dawn this morning. Sunday, members of the Serbian Orthodox faith observed Christmas Eve mass at their church at Idaho and Porphyry Streets. Early this morning, they celebrated the first Christmas mass. At 10 o'clock this morning, they observed the regular Christmas mass.

At all the services, music in the Slavic tongue was furnished by the Young Serb-American group. This group has been trained during the last two months by the Rev. George Milosavijevich, the church's new pastor.

Today the ancient Christmas customs were observed in many of the Serbian homes. Singing upon entering their friends' homes, guests and callers came bearing gifts. All tables in the homes were strewn with hay, a symbol of the surroundings in which Christ was born, and a large, lighted candle was placed in the center of the table, a representation of the star of Bethlehem. At the table, 12 special dishes, representing the 12 apostles, were served, each one being blessed by the head of the house.

To the church in Butte, one of the few Orthodox institutions in the Northwest, came hundreds of members from Anaconda, Philipsburg, Deer Lodge, Helena, Great Falls, and Dillon, to join their Butte colleagues in the yearly holiday observances. Butte did not have the service last year because of the absence of a pastor.

Helena Independent, January 8, 1935

The CCC at Christmas, 1934

The Civilian Conservation Corps (CCC) was created by the Roosevelt Administration in 1933 as an unemployment relief organization. During the next eight years, hundreds of CCC camps were established across the nation—scores of them in Montana, administered from a regional headquarters at Fort Missoula. Many Montana boys enlisted in the CCC, serving both in the state and throughout the West. By the end of 1941, the Corps had employed more than 2,000,000 youths.

$\mathcal{O}$NE HUNDRED FIFTY vacation-bound CCC boys are expected here at 6 p.m. today from the Nine Mile CCC camp.

The lads are the first contingent of Christmas furlough holders. Forty-six are Missoula residents; most of the others will go to Butte, Anaconda, Great

Falls, Kalispell, and other Montana towns. The second division of the camp will be furloughed when the first returns to camp.

At the present time, 520 men are assigned to the three companies in the Nine Mile winter camp. But there are also three "spike" camps, with 50 men on Trout Creek, 50 men on Tank Creek south of Huson, and 32 men on Valley Creek, engaged in road building.

There is a foot of snow on the summit of the reservation divide, where the crews working on the Valley Creek Road are busy. But the snow has not interfered with road building or caused any letup in the advance of the crews. The buildings at the Nine Mile Remount Station, where 11 civilian carpenters are also employed, are rising rapidly.

Missoula Missoulian, December 21, 1934

Christmas Editorial, Lewistown, 1934

Much of what President Franklin D. Roosevelt used to address the economic devastation of the Great Depression was attitude—a spirit of possibility, optimism, and hope. Although the Depression had not yet bottomed out in Montana in 1934, editor Tom Stout of the *Lewistown Democrat-News* echoes Roosevelt's optimistic spirit of promise.

*W*E FEEL SATISFIED that the coming Christmas will come nearer to being a merry one, here and throughout the land, than it has been for some time. Our plight is still very serious, of course, but the improvement over a year ago is now so marked that the blindest partisan cannot deny it. In other ways than the merely material, this change is likewise manifest: it is the change of spirit among the whole people that is most important of all.

The vast majority now has a complete confidence in the leadership of President Roosevelt. It is to him that the changes must be chiefly credited. Confidence in the ability of the government to bring about a return to measurable prosperity, at least, through its policies and its leadership is widespread and seems to be growing all the time. With the present outlook, the people are justified in making this truly a Merry Christmas.

Considering the situation locally, the merchants find that their holiday trade has expanded. Anticipating this, they secured larger, better, and more diversified stocks than usual. These Lewistown stores are quite able to supply the needs of all the shoppers this year.

This confidence of our businessmen deserves to be backed up by the buyers—not only because they certainly cannot gain anything by making purchases elsewhere, but also because this home trade will all make for home prosperity. Do all your trading at home and you will help to make this a Merry Christmas in Lewistown.

Lewistown Democrat-News, December 16, 1934

(left) "Muvver is gettin' off her far-away bunnels, an' I is doin' the lickin' of the seals—my tongue feels sort of withered." *Sonnysayings* cartoon, by F. Y. Cory, December 9, 1931. (right) "At's a good lookin' letter to Santa Claus, Baby, an' we ain't spared the ink none." *Sonnysayings* cartoon, by F. Y. Cory, December 14, 1928. Montana Historical Society Museum, Helena

A Letter to Santa from Wolf Point, 1935

As the Great Depression wore away at national morale, American adults sought a haven from reality in talking motion pictures from Hollywood. When that tendency is combined with a Wolf Point child's imagination at Christmas, it produces a most revealing "Letter to Santa."

*W*ITH CHRISTMAS but a few days away, an influx of letters are being mailed to Santa Claus by the young ones. A number of these letters have been forwarded through the local post office to the home of Santa at the North Pole. One Wolf point kiddie writes:

DEAR SANTA:

On my Christmas vacation, I would like to go out in the country and go skating and sledding. In the house I would play with my doll and buggy and paper dolls and little piano. I would pretend that my Shirley Temple doll was taking piano lessons, then I would play the piano and she would sing. I would have her sing and dance at the Amucher Hour over the radio, and I would have her win. Then I would have her be in the movies. And then I would show the films in the movie machine and pretend that she was a great movie star and everybody thought she was the cutest little girl in the world.

—Your little friend,
XXXXXXXXXXXXXXX

Wolf Point Roosevelt County News, December 18, 1935

Fort Peck Workmen Celebrate, 1936

One of the greatest of Franklin D. Roosevelt's New Deal projects was the construction of the massive, earth-filled Fort Peck Dam on the Missouri River near Glasgow. This project employed thousands of Montanans and brought thousands more outsiders to the state. At the height of construction in 1936, more than 10,500 workers labored on that job. These men and their families settled in makeshift, construction "boom towns" near the dam site. And they too celebrated Christmas of 1936.

*T*HE OLD WEST was rough and tough, but it could have learned something about "real hell-raising" from the mushroom towns clustered about the government's giant Fort Peck Dam project.

Christmas revelry, began last night, continued unabated through today and was still going strong in Wheeler, New Deal, Delano Heights, and the other wide-open boom towns tonight.

There wasn't the gun play that made holiday celebrations hazardous when the West was younger, but the "old days were tame compared to this," said G. W. Kampfer of Glasgow, veteran Justice of the Peace, who bears the cognomen of "Dogie Jack."

Ruby Smith, the queen of Wheeler nightlife, paused from welcoming guests to her gambling tables long enough to tell why the holiday parties were so noisy and long.

"These boys and girls are having their fun while they can," said Ruby. They know it won't last forever. It will all be over here in a year or two; then we'll all drift along.

"Sure we make good money now, but the profits slip away. I've got plenty of 'em on the cuff now—the ones whose jobs and cash ran out."

Over in Fort Peck, the government's model town adjoining the site of the huge earthen dam being thrown across the Missouri river, there was a different Christmas celebration. Fort Peck had a quiet holiday, with even a community Christmas tree.

Wheeler went the model town one better. It had two public trees. One stood before the jail, and the constable assured his one prisoner that there'd be a gift for him from Santa "when your headache lets up."

The other tree was in Ruby's place, and Ruby herself played Santa, inviting the "boys and girls" to step right up to the kegs of free beer.

The soft notes of Christmas hymns were sometimes heard when the roar from the dance hall and gambling houses died down momentarily. Community church services in the fringe towns were all well-attended.

Lewistown Democrat-News, December 26, 1936

[Christmastime in Montana]

Lincoln County Christmas Tree Industry, 1936

The Christmas-tree industry began in northwestern Montana during the 1920s and, by the mid-1930s, was developing into an important Montana business. In its early stages, this industry cut natural trees on private and public lands. Only subsequently did Christmas-tree plantations locate in the area, nurturing trees from planting to harvest. The industry remains a vital component of the forest economy in western Montana.

*F*OR THE PAST SEVERAL YEARS, another industry has been developed in Lincoln County, says the *Western News* of Libby. It is growing from year to year, and few people realize how much money it is turning in to the County. The new industry is the harvesting and sale of Christmas trees.

The newspaper, assisted by Ranger C. R. Byers of the Forest Service, has gathered some statistics that are highly interesting. These are to the effect that 151 carloads of Christmas trees have been shipped or will be shipped out of Lincoln County this year. They are shipped far and wide—to Washington, D.C., into Massachusetts, to St. Louis, Kansas City, and many other eastern and midwestern cities.

Now just what does this business mean to the district in a financial way? First, we have been informed that the freight charges alone will aggregate about $60,000. That's a tidy sum. Inasmuch as the Great Northern Railway is the largest single taxpayer in the county, it can be figured, in a sense, that this $60,000—and more—comes back to County in taxes.

Approximately 600,000 trees have been cut this year, varying in length from 2 to 20 feet. The cutters receive from 2 cents to 15 cents per tree for cutting, yarding, and bundling. This would be approximately $25,000. And $4,800 for the miscellaneous handling and $5,000 for tracking, and one gets some idea of the gross sum that comes into the County from this work. Not figuring anything from the freight charge, there is paid out in wages nearly $35,000. When it is realized that this work comes at a time of the year when labor is beginning to be scarce, its value is all the more appreciated.

Here is additional information regarding this industry that is of interest. There are 4,000 trees to a carload, on the average. The trees are bundled as follows: eight 2-foot trees to a bundle; six 4-foot trees to a bundle; four 6-foot trees to a bundle; three 8-foot trees to a bundle; and two 10-foot trees to a bundle. All trees above 10 feet are shipped singly. The trees are cut from government and private lands.

Some have thought this industry was detrimental, because of the mistaken notion that it might be destroying another natural resource. Ranger Byers says this is not true. In fact, the cutting of trees is really a benefit, as it thins out stands and makes possible the development of better trees. It also clears the ground of less valuable timber, thereby permitting the better development of the more desirable yellow pine. Another factor not often realized is this, states Ranger Byers: Estimated over the length of time it takes the timber to develop, greater income for the Forest Service can be derived per acre from Christmas trees than can be done from the production of sawlogs. Another consideration is the fact that, if properly handled, the Christmas tree industry may continue indefinitely.

Billings Midland Review,
December 26, 1936

A Bitterroot Valley lad posed in front of his decked-out tree. Note the horse-drawn fire engine under the fir. John Westling, photographer, Montana Historical Society Photograph Archives, Helena

Denton Christmas Tree, 1936

In the small, agricultural settlement of Denton, struggling with the seemingly endless Depression, the town's commitment to a community tree and program represents Montanans' strong will to adapt and survive.

𝒯HE DENTON STREETS are taking on a holiday air with an enormous tree which was placed in the center of Broadway Avenue this week. The tree is covered with vari-colored lights which are aglow during the evening. The tree was brought in from the mountains by Ray Lee. A short program is held annually under the tree, and candy is distributed to the children. The tree is sponsored this year by three of Denton's organizations: the American Legion, the Denton Firemen, and the Denton chapter of the Ancient Order of United Workmen.

Lewistown Democrat-News, December 20, 1936

Wolf Point Beautiful for Christmas, 1937

Whatever tragedies and disappointments the Great Depression brought to Montana, it also generated a spirit of community among neighbors faced with often-overwhelming economic forces. That sense of community is evident in Wolf Point in 1937 as this High Line town prepared for Christmas.

*T*HE CHRISTMAS SPIRIT abounds in Wolf Point. The city looks beautiful in its holiday dress; the full length of Assiniboine Avenue is adorned with evergreens. The large community tree arrived the first of the week and has been placed mid-way in the city blocks. It towers to the tops of two-story buildings and looks as natural as if it had grown in its place.

The strings of varied colored lights which criss-cross the streets are augmented by the decorated Christmas trees placed every 25 feet along the Avenue, and when lighted each evening, makes a beautiful sight to behold.

The windows of the stores and shops are all beautifully decorated and lighted in Christmas colors. No metropolitan city can boast of more appropriate, attractive windows than can be seen along the business thoroughfares of Wolf Point.

The business section is not alone in donning the holiday attire.

Throughout the residential section, in every quarter of town, wreaths, Christmas candles and sparkling trees proclaim the holiday season is here, and await in joyful anticipation the coming of the anniversary of the Birth of the Christ Child. It's Christmas Time.

Wolf Point Roosevelt County News, December 16, 1937

Christmas Radio in Wolf Point, 1937

The advent of radio broadcasting in Montana during the 1920s gave way to a proliferation of local radio stations during the 1930s. As the holiday program schedule for KGCX in Wolf Point reveals, Depression-era radio in Montana was particularly local in focus.

*K*GCX WILL PRESENT a number of attractive and appropriate programs on Christmas Eve and on Christmas Day. Friday, from 7:30 to 8:00 o'clock, Miss Florence Tilton will play a program of carols on the electric organ. A note of festiveness will be added by Chy and his Hot Shots, in an hour of dance music from 8:00 to 9:00 p.m. The station leaves the air until midnight, when a broadcast of the Midnight Mass will be made from the Catholic Church, with the Father Francis Shevlin presiding.

On Christmas Day, KGCX presents, from 2:15 to 2:45 p.m., an address from Father Shevlin. From 3:00 to 3:30, Reverend E. C. Kleidon presents a children's Christmas program. The Reverend P. M. Cantelon will be on the air with a musical group from 5:30 to 6:00 p.m. From 6:45 to 7:15 p.m., the American Legion Auxiliary will present a program of selected carols.

Wolf Point Roosevelt County News, December 23, 1937

Christmas with the "Alphabet Agencies," 1938

President Franklin Delano Roosevelt's New Deal programs, designed to employ Americans and to revitalize the national economy, touched every town in Montana. Known as the "alphabet agencies," these programs also assisted communities in maintaining Christmas celebrations during the Depression.

*S*TATE WORKS Progress Administration (WPA) Administrator Joseph E. Parker today revealed that the Montana WPA and the National Youth Administration (NYA) are among Santa Claus' No. 1 assistants this yuletide.

Under regularly established toy projects, principal ones of which are at Havre, Great Falls, and Lewistown, $10,000 was spent by the WPA. About

100 workers were employed the last few months, and several thousand toys were made available to children who otherwise might have spent a giftless Christmas.

In many other cities, a great number of toys were built or improved for distribution by Santa to needy youngsters under the arts-and-crafts activities of the WPA Division of Education and Recreation, and the NYA. Among such places where activities have been extensive are Laurel, Miles City, Columbia Falls, Glendive, and Polson.

In all of the 72 cities, towns, and communities of Montana where the WPA either operates or assists in operating public recreation programs, some type of special Christmas activity—ranging from large Christmas community sings to small Christmas story-telling groups for tots—has been under way this year, Arnold Olson, director of the WPA's Division of Education and Recreation pointed out.

Typical of WPA or NYA efforts throughout the state, Parker said, are activities at Havre. Sufficient toys to care for the city's underprivileged children were produced, with the WPA repairing and the Boy Scouts collecting old toys. The Christmas Cheer Committee of prominent citizens, WPA officials, and civic and other groups conducted an extensive campaign. They collected funds and gift items through donations. The committee gave every needy family a Christmas basket containing food and clothing, and every needy child received candy, fruit, and a gift.

At Lewistown, a large number of toys were built or repaired under a cooperative program in which Boy Scouts, the Fergus County Welfare Department, the city, and the NYA assisted the WPA.

Some 3,000 toys were distributed at Butte, under an NYA toy-repair project sponsored by the Exchange Club, with the assistance of the Camp Fire Girls and the Marian White Arts and Crafts Club. Typical of the WPA's Christmas recreational activities was a community sing and concert attended by several hundred persons. There were three large choirs and several prominent vocalists and other musicians.

The Butte Junior League played host at Christmas parties for some 100 tots enrolled in the city's three WPA nursery schools.

At Missoula, as for many years has been the case, city firemen gathered, repaired, and distributed toys to the needy. At the State University, the spirit of yuletide flowed warmly. Collegiate contributions to Santa took place in the form of a gift party for Missoula's WPA nursery school, given by the Associated Women Students. Baskets were distributed to needy "U" students who are "batching" and working their way through school. In a few cases, financial assistance was contributed for students who met unexpected adversity in finishing the fall quarter.

Darby had a gala public Christmas tree and musical in the public park area completed last summer by the WPA.

At Miles City, the WPA's Recreational Department again organized and directed the street singing of Christmas carols through the business district during the last few rush weeks of Christmas shopping.

Great Falls Tribune, December 25, 1938

Helena Santa Claus, 1938

From 1896 until his death in 1951, A. I. "Daddy" Reeves annually donned his made-to-order costume and played an unconventional Santa Claus to generations of Helena youngsters.

During the rest of the year, the man who became a local institution ran the highly successful Reeves Music Company and was instrumental in bringing internationally known musical performers to Montana. Perhaps "Daddy" Reeves's greatest honor, though, was being known as "a friend of children."

*T*AKE IT FROM a man of experience—this business of playing Santa Claus is no snap and not to be taken lightly.

"Daddy" A. I. Reeves, 74 years old, has been enacting the role of St. Nick for Helena children 41 years without a miss. The way he does it, it's downright violent exercise. He has gone through his routine at community gatherings from two to five times every Christmas week in the last two score years.

"I'm different from the ordinary Santa Claus," "Daddy" says. "I don't play the stale, slow-moving, old-man type."

"Santa Claus is a character from fairy-land so far as little children are concerned, so I act as sprightly as I can throughout a performance. It keeps them excited and interested."

From the time "Daddy" Reeves makes his appearance at a gathering of children until he departs—usually about an hour and a half—he is never still a second, hopping, skipping, jumping, and generally capering all the time.

This routine calls for reserve strength and lots of it.

"I go in training for it every year about Thanksgiving Day," said the pioneer Father Christmas. "Like this—"

Then he does a sort of dog-trot standing in one place.

"I do that 25 steps the first day, then increase the exercise 25 steps a day, until I can keep it up for an hour without losing my breath. I go on a light diet, too."

By Christmas Day, the 74-year-old youngster is in shape to keep the tots' eyes twinkling for an hour and a half with his antics.

Bob Morgan at age nine, Helena, Christmas 1939. Montana Historical Society Photograph Archives, Helena

"The greatest problem in playing Santa Claus is how to cool off," he explains. "After I have danced around and shaken hands with about a thousand children, my underclothing is wringing wet with perspiration.

"It took me 15 years to learn to cool off. Now, when I am through with my acting job, I am blanketed like a race horse and taken home. I get into a tub of warm water and soak for about 30 minutes, then go to bed between warm blankets and remain there for a couple hours. Next I take a cold shower, then I'm ready for a turkey-eating contest."

The Kid Road Agent, by Charles M. Russell (1909). From *Helena Treasure State*, December 18, 1909, Montana Historical Society Library, Helena

"Daddy" Reeves says he has been asked every question a child can think of to ask Santa Claus. His years of experience have taught him to answer every one. When he shakes hands with a youngster he says, in a disguised voice, "Did ye get it?" "What was it?" "I thought ye'd like it."

Children from three to five years of age are the most interest in Santa Claus, "Daddy" Reeves has found. Once some older boys attempted to "expose" "Daddy" Reeves. He sensed that they were going to pull at his beard and clothing so he eluded them and outran the entire group. "It was due to my training that I beat them in the foot race."

His grand entry at a gathering is different every time. It may be down a chimney, on a sleigh, in an auto, or in any other conceivable manner.

"I try to make the entry surprising and funny for the kids," he says. At a children's party several years ago, he lay huddled under a pile of bricks in a fireplace for two hours before he appeared.

Fire destroyed his first Santa Claus suit in 1928. Assembling another was a hard job. For one thing, movies had crowded out the stock companies, and theatrical whiskers and wigs were scarce. He searched for the proper kind all summer and couldn't find one he wanted throughout the entire eastern United States. Finally he located one in San Francisco. It arrived here the day before he was to use it. His suit is made-to-order.

"Daddy" Reeves hires a professional to put on his make-up for the performances.

"I want everything perfect," he says, "just as though I were going out to play Shakespeare."

About the Santa Claus tradition, he says, "I think it's beautiful for a tot to believe in Santa Claus. Why, the old man is one of the chief characters in their fairyland. To deprive a child of the belief makes him old before his time.

"It'll be a blow when they find out it isn't so, but they've got to get used to things like that in this world."

Montana Newspaper Association Insert series, January 3, 1938

War and Recovery

WORLD WAR II, even with all its tragedies—and the dispersal of a significant portion of the state's population—ended decades of economic frustration. The war had infused the federal presence into the lives of home-front Montanans, helping to bring in new money, but also creating a sense of unease. In this climate, the celebration of Christmas assumed new meanings to families.

Montanans enjoyed post-war recovery despite the atom bomb, confusing international relations, and the Cold War. In the process society and Christmas customs experienced a metamorphosis during the Korean conflict and the growing entanglements in Vietnam. Long-standing traditions meshed with new, glitzy customs supported by affluence—except on Indian reservations, where poverty remained a grim constant. The organization Christmas party became a standard, from 4-H clubs to church auxiliaries to sewing circles to women's clubs. Evolving Christmas customs have always marked the Montana holidays.

A Christmas 1945 visit with Santa produced smiles. Montana Historical Society Photograph Archives, Helena

Lambert Christmas News, 1940

In the 1940s, Montanans were not far removed from the community's close observation and control of its schoolteachers. One legacy of this practice was the annual listing of how a town's teachers would spend their Christmas vacations. Such is the case in 1940 in the small ranching community of Lambert in Richland County.

*S*CHOOL CLOSED last Friday for a full two-weeks holiday recess. Each of the rooms presented short, informal programs, and in each gifts were exchanged between pupils. The rooms were unusually well decorated this year.

All Lambert teachers are leaving Lambert for all or part of the holiday vacation. Miss Jacobson and Miss Raudabaugh left Friday evening, the former for her home in Glendive, Miss Raudabaugh to spend two weeks at her home near Corvallis, Montana. Mr. and Mrs. Wilson left Sunday with the Cummings family to drive to Billings. Mr. and Mrs. Wilson will spend about

Shelby Drug decorated for Christmas, 1948. Montana Historical Society Photograph Archives, Helena

a week with Mr. Wilson's family at Lodge Grass, then go to Minot, N. Dak., for a visit with Mrs. Wilson's people. The Cummings family are spending a week at Billings, with Mr. and Mrs. George Dahlgren. Mrs. Vallentine and children will spend most of their vacation at Lambert, but will go to Miles City and Glendive for a few days between Christmas and the New Year.

Several Lambert young people attending college returned home for the holidays last week. Among the first arrivals were Anne and Oscar Kvaalen, and George Howell, of Concordia College, at Moorhead, Minn.; Gordon Holte, of the University of Montana at Missoula; Norman Lindevig of Eastern Montana Normal at Billings; and Anastasia Rehbeing of Northern Montana College at Havre.

Audrey Jarvis, Helen Jacobson, and Eunice Howell, all of whom are teaching in Gallatin County, near Bozeman, returned to Lambert early in the week for the holidays.

Sidney Herald, December 26, 1940

Savage Christmas News, 1941

In the tradition of weekly newspapers located in the county seat, the *Sidney Herald* carried "local happenings" columns written by correspondents in outlying settlements. The village of Savage is situated about 20 miles upstream from Sidney on the Yellowstone River. The Christmas-week column from the Savage correspondent reveals the nature of the wartime holidays in rural Montana.

*M*R. AND MRS. GEORGE BROWNING and daughter, Ruth, of Forsyth spent the Christmas holidays at the John Nelson home. Mr. and Mrs. Charles Nelson and daughter, Marilyn, were also dinner guests at the Nelson home on Christmas day.

Mr. Schultz of near Richey spent Christmas at the home of his sister and family, Mr. and Mrs. Dave McConshe.

Quite a few people of the Savage and Midway communities attended the program held at the Burns School on Tuesday evening, Dec. 23, and enjoyed it very much. Gifts were exchanged and treats were given to all present.

Canine corps sled dogs trained at Rimini, near Helena, in 1943. Montana Historical Society Photograph Archives, Helena

Raymond and Leo Hoffman motored to Williston, N. D., Tuesday to bring their sister, Marie, home with them to spend the holidays at the home of her parents.

The members of the Eastern Star Lodge entertained at a large party at the Masonic Hall on Saturday evening. The hall was beautifully decorated with Christmas decorations. The main attraction was the lunch, which was a smorgasbord. The center piece for this table was a Yule log holding three candles and several little Santa Claus figures standing around it. The committee had gone to very much trouble to make the party a huge success. Games were played during the evening, and also gifts were exchanged. This also was a party to amuse the little folks, whose parents belong to the Lodge.

A very nice Christmas program was presented at the Gospel Mission Church under the direction of Rev. Fenton on Monday evening, and one at the Lutheran Church on Friday evening. Large crowds attended and enjoyed these various Christmas programs.

Mrs. Murray, who has been in the Sidney hospital for the past few days, was able to spend Christmas at her home, but was taken back to the hospital right afterward for further medical attention. Her son, Henry and family of Minneapolis, her two sons, Jim and Alvin of Grand Junction, Colorado, along with other members of her family were here to spend Christmas.

Kenneth Clark joined the United States Army Air Corps on Wednesday and left for a Texas training camp on Sunday.

Sidney Herald, January 1, 1942

Sidney Christmas Drama, 1941

With the advent of World War II, the military services systematically stripped Montana communities of their young men and women. With this depleted population, greater responsibility fell upon the public school to prepare and to perform a Christmas entertainment for the community. This task often presented a problem, since the faculty also had been reduced by the call to arms. One solution was offered in Sidney in 1941.

*S*PONSORED BY the dramatics class, under the direction of Mr. Cook, the third annual Christmas program was presented in the high school auditorium December 17. The theme of the program was "Christmas in Other Lands," and was made up of twelve pantomimes, each with a musical background consisting of solos, a girl's trio, a quartette, and glee clubs.

Beautifully decorated with Christmas greens and lighted to represent the windows of a church, the stage was used as a background for the various scenes as the characters representing different countries, illustrated Christmas customs characteristic of other lands. Christmas customs in the United States were illustrated by a human Christmas tree made up of grade school children in attractive costumes, and a Santa Claus rushing in through the door, jingling bells and throwing candy to the audience. The Glee Club with 87 voices made up the final chorus.

The program, managed entirely by the dramatics class, is the school's gift to the community. Credit for its success is due to everyone who participated in it.

Sidney Herald, December 18, 1941

Greetings for Liberty County Soldiers, 1942

The degree to which Montanans, and Americans from coast to coast, threw themselves into the consuming effort to supply the Allied war effort between 1941 and 1945 was remarkable. Not only did those folks on the home front make daily sacrifices, they worked diligently to encourage members of the military around the globe. This dedication is reflected in a Christmas message from the High Line in 1942.

*T*O THE YOUNG MEN from Liberty County now serving in the armed forces:

We, your loved ones at home, salute you, and send you greetings this Christmas season.

We want you to know that we will be thinking about you as we gather around our firesides to celebrate this Christmas season, the most precious festivity of all the year. We will miss you, of course, but we are proud of the job you are doing and the sacrifices you are making. We know that you will be better men and citizens as a result of your unselfish service to your country. When the war has been won, you will the better fitted for the tremendous task ahead in helping to rebuild this shattered world.

We, whose lot it has been to stay at home and keep things going as best we can, will not fail you. Sometimes we feel our part is small and inconsequential, compared to yours. But we know that not all men can serve in the armed forces, any more than all can remain at home in comparative safely and comfort, while you younger men go forth to battle for the preservation of the homeland, the ideals and institutions we all cherish even above life itself.

Our prayer is that you be given full strength to carry out the task at hand to a successful conclusion, and that when the victory is won it will be yours to return safely to your beloved homeland and carry through to the attainment of that ideal condition in this world proclaimed by angels two thousand years ago when they visioned "Peace on earth, among men of good will."

The little inconveniences we are undergoing here at home are as nothing. We apologize to you for the petty quibbling and complaining we are sometimes wont to indulge in because of a shortage of a few spoonsful of sugar or coffee or a few gallons of gasoline. These things are not sacrifices, and are not even worthy of being called inconveniences. Yours is the real sacrifice and service, and we want you to know we appreciate it. Again we salute you and greet you and wish you luck.

Chester Liberty County Times, December 24, 1942

Wartime Christmas Radio, 1943

In the 1940s, commercial radio in Montana had developed to the stage where many local stations could tie into national radio networks. This technological advance proved particularly useful in obtaining reports from the various fronts and in creating a sense of unity between wartime efforts on the home front and overseas. Those relationships became a significant part of the dark Christmas of 1943 for many Montanans.

$\mathcal{O}$N CHRISTMAS DAY, men and women of the American Armed Forces in every quarter of the globe will hear three hours of special Christmas radio programs. They will feature entertainment stars, name bands, and personal greetings from the Secretary of War, the Secretary of the Navy, and high officers from the various other service branches.

On Christmas Eve and on Christmas Day, the people on the home front will hear programs from soldiers overseas. These programs will include a chorus of 200 American soldiers in the Holy Land, a Christmas tree decorating from an island in the South Pacific, and Midnight Mass from some place behind the battle lines in Italy.

Sidney Herald, December 23, 1943

Christmas in Pella and Brorson, 1943

The small Danish communities of Pella and Brorson are located several miles to the northwest of Sidney, in Richland County. During World War II, these churches were served each week by the Reverend Henry N. Hansen from Sidney. In 1943 Reverend Hansen wrote the following column to inform his parishioners of the Christmas-season schedule. Because of the preponderance of Danish members in these congregations, special arrangements were made to honor traditions brought from Denmark.

$\mathcal{C}$HRISTMAS EVE, December 24, is celebrated at home or in visiting with relatives and friends. The Christmas tree is lit for the first time, and Christmas gifts are exchanged.

Christmas Day, December 25, brings festival services in the churches. A special Christmas message is brought by the pastor. There is special music and Christmas anthems by the choir.

The Sunday schools have their Christmas-tree festivals, at Pella on December 26 at 7:30 p.m., and at Brorson on December 27 at 1:00 p.m. All the children in the Sunday schools have a part in the Christmas programs.

The young people in the Brorson church will have their Christmas party at the parsonage on Wednesday, December 29. Caroling is an old custom. The young people of the Pella church will sing for the sick, the shut-ins, and the feeble on Christmas Day evening. This will be followed by a Christmas party at the parsonage.

Neither are the older members of the congregation forgotten at Christmas. A Danish Christmas service will be held on Sunday, December 26, at 2:30 p.m.—and again on Tuesday, December 28, at 7:30 p.m. The Danish Christmas festival, sponsored by the ladies of the church, will be celebrated with a

Children at the Union Bank and Trust Company's annual Christmas party, Helena, December 22, 1953. L. H. Jorud, photographer, Montana Historical Society Photograph Archives, Helena

service in the church, when Pastor Niels Damskov will bring the message. This will be followed by a social hour in the church parlors, where refreshments will be served by the Ladies Aid.

Pastor Henry N. Hansen will broadcast over KGCX, a Christmas Day message on Christmas Day, from 7:30 until 8:00 p.m. A most blessed Christmas season to all!

Sidney Herald, December 23, 1943

Charley Creek Christmas News, 1943

The Charley Creek drainage sits on the south side of the Missouri River, in northern Richland County, right across the river from the Brockton area. World war or no world war, the people who inhabited this hauntingly beautiful stock country during the early 1940s maintained their holiday traditions through their schools and through the gathering of families, regardless of the inconveniences involved.

*L*ITTLE GLORIA and LeRoy Fisher have been ill with the measles the past two weeks so the William Fishers were unable to attend any of the Christmas programs.

Lena Grace Thompson gave a very nice program and tree at the Armstrong School Wednesday evening. She just completed a summer term of school and will return in March to teach another term.

Mrs. William Fehrs entertained the community at a nice tree and program at the Ruffatto School Thursday evening.

The children and their teacher, Mrs. Antone Schmitz, gave a little program and party at the Fisher School Friday afternoon. Those coming were Avis Schmitz, Mrs. Harry Hagen and Judy, Mrs. William Ralston, Mrs. Bailey Fisher, and Mrs. Leonard Smith. Mrs. Schmitz gave candy for prizes in games in which all took part, then she served ice cream cones and Christmas cookies.

Howard Smith and Edgar Fisher drove around by the Culbertson bridge to Brockton to get Edward Smith to bring him home for vacation, as the ice was floating in the river, making a 130-mile trip where it's only 3 miles from the Smith home to Brockton.

Mr. and Mrs. Steve Ruffatto and son John went to Sidney Christmas Eve after their daughter Lucy.

Sidney Herald, December 30, 1943

Christmas Editorial from Whitefish, 1943

At the height of the war effort—being fought on two fronts, in Europe and the Pacific—the Christmas of 1943 provided an opportunity for thoughtful Americans to reflect on their national situation. The editor of the *Whitefish Pilot*, G. M. Moss, took that occasion to look beyond the Allied effort to a post-war world.

TOMORROW IS CHRISTMAS in the Year of Our Lord 1943. It is a difficult Christmas. It is hard to preserve an attitude of good cheer and good will in a world largely dominated by hate and destruction. One cannot but wonder what the Prince of Peace would say if He could give a new message to the world.

Neither can any thoughtful person avoid wondering where the great failure has been. Have our religious teachers failed? Have our social and political teachers failed? Have they all failed?

Is the human race so delicately balanced between good and evil that a few neurotics and egomaniacs can, in a few days, turn the whole world into a chamber of horrors? Is this thing we call civilization just a thin coating for primitive savagery?

The big thing, of course, is a complete Victory by the forces of right over the forces of evil and wickedness, before another Christmas shall have come. But when Victory comes, where are we going—back to the old plans and policies that will nurture another global horror?

The leaders of the post-war world have a heavy responsibility. It cannot be met by playing power politics—by territorial grabs—by a frantic scramble for trade advantages. It cannot be met without the inspiration of a Power higher than any earthly power—and that is the only meaning that Christmas 1943 can have to the adult mind. Truly, the highest hopes of humanity hang in the balance.

Whitefish Pilot, December 24, 1943

Richland County Soldier Writes Home, 1944

One of the wartime contributions of Charlie Hurly, the *Sidney Herald* editor from 1926 to 1958, was to provide every Richland County man and woman in the service with a free subscription to the hometown newspaper, regardless of where they were stationed in the world. This gift elicited numerous letters from servicemen abroad, which Hurly then published in his paper, maintaining ties between the home front and the various theaters of war.

Southwest Pacific Area
December 7, 1944

 EAR MR. HURLY:

I have been going to write for a long time and let you know that we get the *Herald* OK. Calvin Sowle and myself are still together since we left home in March 1941. I don't think we have missed over a half dozen copies of the *Herald* in over 30 months down here. Uncle Sam takes pretty good care of us boys' mail, it seems.

I would like to be home for Christmas, but it looks like another one down here, making three of them so far. While I write this, I have to stop and wipe about a pint of sweat off my brow every minute or two. I just got a letter from home saying it was around 15 below zero up there; that would be quite a change for me.

I have heard of rotation and furloughs for a long time, but one never knows what the score is. They say all things to come to those who wait, so I am waiting. I am thankful I am still in good repair so far anyway. The grub is plentiful, and we hear most of the war news sooner or later. I have a little change of address I will put below.

I think this is plenty for this time, so will quit. Hope this finds you as frisky as it leaves me.

—Pfc. Sidney M. Bower

Sidney Herald, December 21, 1944

Sidney Christmas Greetings, 1944

Sidney Herald editor Charles Hurly used that same Christmas to write an editorial of reason and hope in a world of chaos.

*H*OLLY ON THE DOOR and a candled wreath in the window. Stockings by the fireplace, carols in the dark, and the jeweled Christmas tree glittering through the night. What would Christmas be without them?

The answer is . . . it would still be Christmas.

For Christmas isn't symbols . . . Christmas is something that happens to people. It wells up, overflows, bursts forth from the heart of every human being. It goes far beyond the traditional forms of our American observance . . . adopts a hundred different forms all over the world and transcends them all. Christmas is the sweetest emotional experience shared at one time by mankind.

There's not a flake of snow in the South Pacific tonight, not a single tinkling sleigh bell. But the tender joy of Christmas fills fighting American hearts on every atoll and palm-fringed isle. There are no street singers in the North Atlantic, nor a Christmas tree in all its watery waste of miles. The men on the icy convoys need no symbols to remind them . . . their thoughts and love and prayers tonight are winging home to you.

So let not the absence of a loved one depress you or steal your holiday joy. The Spirit of Christmas is working in his heart as in yours; he is sharing your Christmas with you just as certainly as if he were greeting you in the glow of your own lighted tree—as he will, most assuredly, on a Christmas yet to come.

Sidney Herald, December 21, 1944

Mansfield Sends Christmas Greetings, 1944

Mike Mansfield endures as Montana's consummate politician and statesman. In 1944 he was serving his first term in the U.S. House of Representatives. He would be a member of Congress for the next 33 years, rising to the position of Senate Majority Leader (1961–1977). Mansfield subsequently served as the U.S. Ambassador to Japan from 1977 to 1989.

$\mathcal{C}$ONGRESSMAN MIKE MANSFIELD, who is in China as a special envoy of the President of the United States, joins the service men in sending greetings.

Congressman Mansfield, who represents the western Montana district, and whose home is in Missoula, recently conferred with high-ranking members of the Chinese government, and will report directly to President Roosevelt on his return to Washington, which is expected soon after the first of the year.

Chester Liberty County Times, December 21, 1944

Chester Christmas Greetings, 1944

Chester, county seat of Liberty County, serves as the marketing center for a surprisingly large portion of northern Montana. In 1944 the editor of the *Liberty County Times*, Thomas A. Busey, acknowledged the strengthening Montana economy, rebounding in wartime from its Depression nadir.

$\mathcal{M}$ANY OF THE business places of Chester and Joplin are this week extending Christmas greetings through the columns of the *Liberty County Times* and, in this proffer of good wishes, this newspaper joins most sincerely.

As we come to the close of a busy, and with most of us a successful year, it is only fitting that we pause at this happy Christmas time to extend to each other the greetings of the season.

Christmas this year, as in the past several years, will be saddened for many by the absence of loved ones, many of whom are on the far-flung battlefields of the world or are away in various ways serving their country in the crucial war effort. But for those of us who must needs remain at home, it would serve no useful purpose to refrain from the joyousness that traditionally prevails throughout the world at Christmas time.

The celebration of the Christmas this year will doubtless be more sober and restrained than in former years, but there should and will be wholesome and joyous exchanges of greetings and felicitations, and the strengthening of ties of love and friendships characteristic of the year-end holiday season.

Chester Liberty County Times, December 21, 1944

A World War II Christmas in Great Falls, 1945

During World War II, Great Falls developed a significant military population attached to East Base, the precursor of Malmstrom Air Force Base. Although V-E Day had been celebrated on May 8 and V-J Day on August 15 of 1945, a wartime atmosphere pervaded the Christmas holidays of that year.

*P*ATIENTS AT THE Army Air Base Hospital in Great Falls may be a long way from home this Christmas, but they have not been forgotten. For the last week, they have been entertained with Christmas programs presented by various clubs of the city, under the auspices of the Camp and Hospital Council of the American Red Cross.

Christmas morning gifts will be distributed to the men by Santa Claus, represented by one of the convalescent patients, in a cutter made of a hospital cart dressed up in cardboard runners.

Many of the patients have been invited to private homes for Christmas dinners, but for those not able to go, there will be turkey and all the trimmings served at the hospital.

Groups entertaining at the hospital last week included Girl Scouts, Camp Fire Girls, College of Education co-eds, Veterans of Foreign Wars auxiliary, and the Kiwanis Club.

Great Falls Tribune, December 24, 1945

Christmas Notes from the Hardin Editor, 1947

Beginning in 1947, the Christmas editorials in Montana weekly newspapers adopted a little bit lighter tone. Although Montanans had to rationalize life with the atom bomb and to understand confusing international politics, World War II was over and the Allies had emerged victorious. In the conversational column of Helen M. Peterson, the editor of the *Hardin Tribune-Herald*, that tone of tentative relaxation is evident. Montana slowly would return to "normal"— whatever that was.

𝓗ARDIN put on her holiday attire this week. Strings of colored lights, covered with evergreen branches, neon stars, and a big tree on the courthouse lawn were put up last weekend by city employees.

Detour signs re-route large trucks whose tops would strike and tear down the decorations.

The city released a list of those who contributed toward the decorations and toward a Christmas treat for the children following a free picture show at the Harriet Theatre on Saturday.

It was pointed out that those who were asked to donate for the Halloween party were not requested to give, since funds left over from that earlier project were used for the decorations and the treats.

We heard this week about an old superstition in connection with Christmas that is new to us. We don't know its origin, or how widespread it is, but we think it is interesting.

Western Life Insurance Company Christmas party, Helena, December 21, 1950. L. H. Jorud, photographer, Montana Historical Society Photograph Archives, Helena

This is it: If you would have a full larder and plenty to eat during the coming year, give food as a Christmas gift or feed someone on Christmas Day. We understand that having guests at Christmas dinner fulfills the requirements—or the customary fruitcake or box of candy will do the trick too.

We wonder how many people there are in this community who have heard of this custom, perhaps as children; we're also curious about the whys and wherefores of this tradition. There is usually a reason of some sort behind most superstitions.

Baby Howard McGee's first Christmas, December 29, 1949. Warren McGee, photographer, Montana Historical Society Photograph Archives, Helena

On this basis, there is one man in Hardin who should be well-fed, if there is anything to this idea of giving food. He is W. J. Brock, and he told us that he'll have a sack of candy and fruit for every grade-school child in Hardin in the week between Christmas and New Year's.

Mr. Brock says that he didn't have much candy himself as a child, and that he's always glad to see the kids make plentiful purchases. Enough in the way of sweets is something every boy and girl should have once in a while, he feels. We think that maybe he's right. We were rationed on this candy proposition ourselves in our youth, because (we were told) a tummy ache might be the result. We never did get enough candy to find out whether it would cause said tummy ache. But we always felt that it would be worth it, just once, to see.

But to get back to Mr. Brock—we distinctly remember, in the days during the war, when you couldn't get a candy bar for love nor money, he managed to keep enough from his allotment to give one to all the kids in town during the holidays.

Hardin Herald-Tribune, December 18 and 25, 1947

Billings Christmas Message, 1948

As the American industrial complex retooled after the concerted effort required by World War II, Montanans joined somewhat in the incipient wave of economic prosperity. After years of depression and self-denial, worry about growing materialism accompanied this prosperity. The cry of a "commercialized Christmas" again was heard in the land, as it had been during the 1890s and in the years before World War I. In 1948 the editor of the *Billings Gazette* selected that subject for his Christmas editorial.

*T*HE PRESENT-DAY celebration of Christmas has swung to an extreme. Like most of our other holidays—Fourth of July, Thanksgiving, Mother's Day—it has lost most of its original significance for great numbers of people by becoming grossly commercialized. Much of the comment one hears as the date of the observance approaches has to do with the number and total value of sales made through commercial channels. The volume of those sales has become an index, not to growing reverence attached to the occasion, but to indicate the state of the country's business health.

But Christmas does, nevertheless, afford an opportunity for giving expression to some of the most generous impulses of the human heart. The exchange of gifts is a manifestation of those attributes of sincere respect, friendship, and affection which make the civilized person. Even though many do not recognize it, the very atmosphere of Christmas is redolent of an odor of sanctity and lifts any person of normal sensibilities up to a high, though perhaps temporary, plane of thinking and inspires a more tolerant relationship with his fellows.

The sum total of that outpouring of kindliness and thoughtfulness and compassion, which is exhibited by the vast numbers of packages sent to less fortunate people in other lands, is a true manifestation of the spirit which should mark the observance of Christmas. It warms the hearts of the givers no less than those of the recipients. It is a demonstration of our belief in, and acceptance of the life and teaching of Him whose birth and teachings we celebrate at this Christmas festival.

Billings Gazette, December 25, 1948

A Postwar Christmas in Billings, 1948

Although postwar international relations did not permit Americans to regain a sense of a pacified world, Christmas celebrations in the late 1940s offered a respite from global warfare. The country's slow reorientation to business and personal pursuits is reflected in the Christmas that Billings residents enjoyed in 1948.

*T*HE STAR OF BETHLEHEM shone over Billings on Friday night, as it shone over the Manger nearly 2,000 years ago.

Then, as now, it shone on a world divided, but Christians everywhere will unite this Christmas Day in a prayer for "Peace on earth, good will towards men."

In keeping with tradition, Billings residents will exchange gifts, worship the Savior at the church of their choice, and gather around the festive board with their families and friends.

All signs on Friday pointed to a joyous holiday for everyone in the city. Needy families were assured of a share in the celebration, as the Family Welfare Service completed the distribution of food baskets to more than 200 families, along with toys for 425 children.

The homeless, too, will not be forgotten. Salvation Army officers announced that preparations were being made to provide Christmas dinner for about 100 transients and persons without friends or relatives with whom to spend the day. Roast beef, plum pudding, and fresh fruit highlight the menu, Major A. E. Austin said.

Children at the two hospitals received a long-awaited visit from St. Nicholas early on Friday evening, and the Red Cross Gray Ladies gave a party for the youngsters on Friday afternoon.

Church groups, Brownie Girls Scouts, and singers from Billings Senior High School and from Central Catholic High have been serenading hospital patients for the last week, hospital officials reported.

Billings Gazette, December 25, 1948

Billings Christmas Seal Campaign, 1949

One of the most visible post–World War II Christmas charity drives involved the American Tuberculosis Association and its Christmas Seal campaign. Not only were these annual fund-raisers highly successful, but they also showed the adaptation of a wartime practice to a peacetime campaign.

*T*UBERCULOSIS SEAL sales had reached $8,757.32 by Saturday as the official "Dove of Peace" campaign drew to a close for Yellowstone County, Peter Yegen, Jr., county drive chairman, announced. The County's goal is $12,000.

Mrs. O. R. Burdette, Laurel campaign chairman, reported $850 had been received there by Saturday. Replies are expected to a number of letters in the area after Christmas, she said.

Members of the Camp Fire Girls mailed Christmas seals for the American Lung Association, November 9, 1953. L. H. Jorud, photographer, Montana Historical Society Photograph Archives, Helena

The Billings headquarters, from which letters were sent to all but Laurel residents of the County, is expected to receive replies in the weeks following Christmas, Yegen said.

Last year's final returns totaled $11,359, Mrs. Helen Robbins, Yellowstone County Tuberculosis Association secretary, said. The final pre-Christmas count for 1948 was $9,147.52, she said.

Senior-high-school typing students prepared 1949 seal-sale letters. Billings Girl Scouts prepared envelopes for mailing, and Boy Scouts placed campaign posters in the city.

Laurel campaign activities were handled through the Laurel Woman's Club, assisted by Girl Scouts of Troop 1.

Billings Gazette, December 25, 1949

Korean War Editorial from Columbia Falls, 1950

The post–World War II Cold War heated up considerably during 1950 when North Korean Communist forces, armed with Soviet-made weapons, invaded South Korea. In the resulting "police action," American troops fought under the aegis of the United Nations. Between 1950 and 1953, more than 33,000 Americans were killed in this war. On the home front, the Korean conflict never gained widespread popular support—at least in part because it followed so quickly World War II. Pulitzer Prize recipient Mel Ruder, of the *Hungry Horse News* in Columbia Falls, confronts this difficulty in his Christmas editorial for 1950.

*A*MERICANS apparently prefer to become excited about a war only once in each generation.

The Korean conflict, with the involvement of China and Russia, comes too soon after World War II to get us beating drums and making speeches. The result is that, where Pearl Harbor caused a mighty onrush of flag-waving and emotion, the more destructive Korean campaign is treated as an aftermath or as a prelude, and not legitimately as the "real thing."

The bloody conflict, however, is hitting home. And there's a score of Flathead Valley families whose Christmas this year is emptier for the loss of young men fallen in battle. Yet the nation does not admit that there's another war.

Lt. Paul Smithey, the son of Mr. and Mrs. P. T. Smithey of Columbia Falls, wrote his sister, Mrs. Eugene Lance, a vivid letter about Korea.

The Smitheys here know there is a war. Paul picked up two bullet holes in his parka coming out from Chosin Reservoir, suffered frost bite, and now is in an Osaka, Japan, hospital recovering from pneumonia.

He wrote a story of 34 truckloads retreating from near the Yalu River. Once, the infantry detachment (which had just eight officers) was under fire all night. On the next morning, Paul walked around the perimeter and counted about 700 Chinese dead. Some of the Chinese didn't have rifles and were armed with just one hand grenade each. Life in China is cheap.

The American detachment finally became mired in mud, out of gas, and without ammunition. Paul and a South

Howard McGee and his new engine, December 30, 1951. Warren McGee, photographer, Montana Historical Society Photograph Archives, Helena

Korean runner then left cross country in zero weather to reach a Marine group known to be five miles away. He used the compass his dad had given him here in Montana. Paul reached the Marines and, later, the infantry detachment with its mired trucks was relieved.

The path toward peace is not a leisurely walk, enjoying the comforts and privileges of a free and prosperous democracy. The nation's mind is not focused on pulling in its belt. Leaders in Washington inspire no particular confidence. Wouldn't it be just fine if there weren't an enemy this Christmas?

Columbia Falls Hungry Horse News, December 22, 1950

Few Letters to Santa from Butte, 1952

Although the writing of letters to Santa Claus at Christmas really gathered momentum after World War II, few American children penned such requests to Santa in 1952—for reasons that have defied the explanation of social historians.

*O*UT OF AN estimated 2,000,000 letters and greetings that poured through the post office in Butte since the first of December, only nine letters were addressed to Santa Claus, North Pole, it was reported Wednesday by Postmaster Joseph E. Parker.

And of those nine letters, only three bore return addresses or identified the writer. None of the letters was extravagant in requests for toys, Postmaster Parker said. The letters were turned over to Butte organizations for investigation and delivery of toys, if the need was found great.

Usually, the postmaster reported, Santa's mail is quite heavy. This year the volume has been light, not only in Butte but in other communities from all parts of the country. In Baltimore, Maryland, for example, it was reported that only one letter out of an estimated 10,000,000 was addressed to Santa.

Butte Montana Standard, December 25, 1952

A Massive Christmas Display in Meaderville, 1953

The town of Meaderville, originally a smelter community on the east end of the Butte Hill, was tied to Butte with a street-railway line. By the turn of the century, Meaderville had become an Italian settlement that, during Prohibition, featured nationally renowned speakeasies and gambling houses. The elaborate Christmas displays created by the Meaderville Volunteer Fire Department garnered the community similar renown after World War II. Unfortunately, Meaderville subsequently became the victim of the Berkeley open-pit mining operation.

*A*N IMPRESSIVE seven-spired cathedral has risen in Meaderville, glowing with brilliant illumination that switches from conventional to black light, to give dramatic emphasis to a central nativity scene. The structure is the

1953 Christmas display of the Meaderville Volunteer Fire Department, and it is even more striking than any of those which have focused national attention on Meaderville in past yuletides.

The display is 36 feet in height and 50 feet in width. The spires are outlined with colored lights and inlaid by illuminated "windows" which silhouette the figures of apostles and the Madonna and child. However, the entire cathedral front is background to the motif which appears in a cutout through the central portion of the display, shaped like a Christmas tree with lighted candles at the tip of each branch. The inset interior highlights a portrait of Mary and the Christ Child, under the brilliance of the Star from the East. Shepherds in attitudes of wonder and adoration cluster about.

The switch from conventional to black light plays up the scene and the Christmas story written in the panels bordering it: "She brought forth her firstborn son and wrapped him in swaddling clothes and laid him in a manger. An angel appeared unto the shepherds keeping watch over their flocks at night. The angel said, 'Fear not. I bring you tidings of great joy, for born unto you this day is a savior which is Christ the Lord.'"

The entire display is balanced by side panels in each of which chimes ring out through the carols played from a recorder inside the Fire Hall. The words "Merry Christmas" shine from the bottom of the billboard, and silvered evergreens stand at either side.

The spectacular display represents untold hours of planning and an estimated 2,040 man-hours of actual work for the ingenious Meaderville firemen, led by Chief Robert Brown. Members working at night put in 1,560 man-hours in the initial building of the display and another 480 hours placing it in position outside. In all, they gave six full weeks of their leisure time to construct their Christmas greeting.

The materials with which they built their cathedral include from 2,000 to 2,100 square feet of wallboard covering the framework, some 1,500 square feet of lumber, and literally miles of wiring. All the back wall is winterized. The "greeting card" utilizes approximately 24,000 watts. It requires three 100-amp boxes and about 400 globes of various sizes and colors. There are nine 1,000 watt spot lights.

Butte Montana Standard, December 20, 1953

Christmas at the St. Ignatius Mission Church, 1954

The Jesuits founded St. Ignatius Mission in the Flathead Valley in 1854, shortly after the creation of St. Mary's Mission in the Bitterroot Valley. The current Catholic church, noted for its resplendent frescoes, was built in 1891—the year after the Ursuline nuns arrived to begin teaching to local Native children.

*T*HE TRADITIONAL midnight mass at the Mission Church was followed by two masses. At the second, the Indians sang hymns. On Christmas morning, masses were said at 8:00 and 10:00. Father Taelman spoke in the Salish Indian language at the latter mass.

Children who remained at the Ursuline Convent over Christmas were the recipients of treats and gifts from several groups, among which were: the Fort Connah Business and Professional Women, St. Ignatius; a sorority group at Bozeman; the Elks of Polson; several groups from the University campus at Missoula. The Elks of Missoula took the children to that city for a movie, and each child was given a large bag containing an orange, an apple, candy, and a toy. Another group from Missoula came to the convent with entertainment and Christmas stockings.

St. Ignatius Post, December 30, 1954

Wolf Point Christmas Crisis, 1954

Wolf Point residents, like most Montanans, planned to spend Christmas in traditional ways in 1954—until that choice was taken out of their hands. "The best laid schemes o' mice an' men. . . ."

*R*ESIDENTS OF south Wolf Point were without water most of last Saturday [Christmas Day] and Sunday, and Christmas dinners were delayed after a break occurred in an eight-inch water main just south of Highway No. 2 on Fourth Avenue North. The main carried water directly from the pumps to the tanks.

A section of the cast-iron pipe, originally installed in 1917, had worn through or rotted, allowing the water to follow an obsolete tile sewer toward the Farmer Lumber Company.

Water service would have been restored about 10 a.m. Saturday except for another unfortunate occurrence. When the city engineer attempted to turn off the valve near the Sijenberg Implement Company, he found it impossible because of its rusted condition. Closing the valve would have permitted pumping water to the southside homes. A replacement for the valve is now in the process of being installed.

The main was believed to have broken about 10 p.m. Friday, but was not discovered until early the next morning after the water had risen through a crack in the cement flooring at the lumber company.

Water also rose to the surface of the gutter on the east side of the highway, forcing the pavement two feet into the air and causing a number of breaks.

Searching for the main break, the city work crew dug 11½ feet down through the frozen ground and then started digging toward the south. When no break was found, the water valve was turned on again, and the men discovered they had been digging in the wrong direction.

J. Hugo Aronson driving a snow plane near Jackson, February 1956. Montana Historical Society Photograph Archives, Helena

A permanent sleeve was placed around the broken main making water service available again, until a second break occurred just a few feet from the first, causing additional delay.

After completion of repair work to the valve, water service was restored thirty-six hours after the city was first notified.

A similar break occurred less than a half-block from the location of the recent breakage during the coldest weather last winter. With temperature hitting as low as 57 degrees below zero, four days elapsed before the water main could be repaired.

Wolf Point Herald-News, December 30, 1954

Deer Lodge Home Decoration Contest, 1954

Decorating the exteriors of residences began during the post–World War II period in Montana. By the 1950s, a number of communities in the state were sponsoring contests to encourage this highly visible celebration of the Christmas season. In Deer Lodge, this practice was well established by 1954.

THE CHRISTMAS home-decorating arrangement at the home of Mr. and Mrs. Harold Gustafson, 712 Carter Street, won first place and a prize of $15 in the annual contest sponsored jointly by the Powell County Civic Association and the Deer Lodge Bank and Trust Company.

Second prize went to Mr. and Mrs. Louis Plett, 831 Pennsylvania Avenue.

Prizes of $5 each were awarded to Mr. and Mrs. Francis Koehnke, 1013 Milwaukee Avenue; Mr. and Mrs. Robert Hickman, 906 Kentucky Avenue; Mr. and Mrs. Ralph Periman, 902 Peterson Avenue; and Mrs. and Mrs. George Peck, 1106 Fourth Street.

Two juveniles, Maurice Wilson and Joe Grover, tied for a $5 prize.

The Gustafsons' first-prize winner was a manger scene using life-size characters. Inside an open stable stood a small manger in which the Christ Child lay, His mother hovering over Him and His father, Joseph, standing nearby. Real hay lay in a heap along one wall. Outside, under floodlights, the Three Wise Men approached across the lawn. Figures had been cut from plywood and painted. At either upper corner of the stable, small white angels stood, with wings outspread, bright stars over their heads.

The Plett second-prize winner showed a four-foot-tall white angel, a wide halo around his head, standing in a mass of blue light. On either side there were six tall red candles, graduating in height from 54 inches to 26 inches. All stood before a large picture-window studded with dozens of bright stars.

The Koehnkes' arrangement occupies the entire front porch. There was a tiny lighted church, on the front of which was a glowing picture of Jesus' face. A small tree was trimmed with multicolored lights, and a row of blue lights interspersed with greenery outlined the eaves. Back of the arrangement, a bright star shone from a picture window.

At the Hickman home, Santa Claus and his reindeer moved across the ground at the rear of the grounds. In the front of them stood two lighted Christmas trees and a small lighted house.

There were so many excellent arrangements, said the committee, that is was difficult to choose any for special recognition. Designs ranged from simple lighted wreaths in windows or doorways to colorfully lighted trees of all sizes and combinations of greenery and lights.

Deer Lodge Silver State Post, December 31, 1954

Prison Christmas Dinner, 1955

The Montana State Prison has operated in Deer Lodge since 1889. During the 1950s, overcrowding placed severe pressure on the facility, resulting in a 1957 riot and death. On the occasion of Christmas Day, however, special efforts were made by the prison staff to provide a traditional holiday meal.

$\mathcal{I}$NMATES OF MONTANA STATE PRISON will be among the well-fed in the community when Christmas Day comes along. Their menu will consist of just about everything that one usually associates with Christmas eating.

Heading the menu will be roast turkey. This will be accompanied by oyster dressing, cranberry sauce, giblet gravy, lettuce-tomato-celery-nut

Rothe Hall Toy Shop, Montana State Prison, Deer Lodge. Montana Historical Society Photograph Archives, Helena

salad, candied yams, relish, ripe olives, sweet and dill pickles, parkerhouse rolls, pumpkin pie, coffee (with milk and sugar, if desired), candy, and nuts.

Christmas Day feasting will start with breakfast in the morning, when the men and women will be served fried ham, scrambled eggs, hot biscuits and butter, iced peaches, oranges, bread, coffee, milk and sugar.

Because of the elaborate dinner and breakfast, only two meals will be served that day.

Deer Lodge Silver State Post, December 23, 1955

Santa Comes to Chester, 1957

By 1957 the businessmen of the agricultural-supply community of Chester had developed a successful strategy to increase Christmas sales on the High Line.

$\mathcal{S}$ANTA CLAUS ARRIVED via Shetland pony-drawn wagon Saturday afternoon. He was greeted with cheers, hugs, and kisses by local children. Jovial old St. Nick handed out treats to all the small fry. There was plenty left over after everyone received a treat.

Then, in an unexpected move, Santa gave all the children a special thrill. He gave them all rides in his wagon. The kids had a wonderful time, and so did Santa.

Cooperating with Santa, Chester stores stayed open until 9 p.m. Saturday night to afford people a chance to do Christmas shopping. The streets were lined with cars all day, and right up until 9 p.m. there were customers in the Christmas shopping centers.

Chester Liberty County Times, December 19, 1957

Chester Christmas School Program, 1957

By the 1950s the tradition of a Christmas-tree celebration in the one-room school had developed into a significant Christmas program at the local high school, as exemplified in this newspaper account from Chester.

$\mathcal{O}$NE OF THE BIGGEST crowds ever to assemble under one roof in Chester greeted the Chester High School band when it opened the Christmas program from the stage in the auditorium Wednesday night. Practically every seat in the auditorium was occupied and the multi-purpose room had an overflow crowd practically all evening.

The band played three numbers, "Keynoter March" by Erickson, "Highlights from the King and I" by Rogers and Hammerstein II, and "A Merry Christmas" by Frangkiser. As usual, the program was well received and was very much appreciated by the audience.

Miss Helen Balls then directed the Junior High School Mixed Chorus in "Oh Holy Night" by Heartz, with Terry Rockman taking the solo.

In the absence of Mrs. Norada Paxton, Mrs. Ruth Barrett directed the High School Mixed Chorus in "A Flemish Carol" and the High School Boys Chorus in "While Shepherds Watched" by Walter Ehret.

Then the stage was set for the presentation of "Heigh-Ho Holly," a Christmas operetta presented by the boys and girls in the Primary and Intermediate grades of the Chester schools.

A festive Christmas tree and gifts in a Helena home provided holiday cheer. Montana Historical Society Photograph Archives, Helena

It would not be possible to name all the characters in this operetta in the time and space allotted. It is enough to say that the operetta was well presented by the youngsters, they got a great big thrill out of putting it on, seemed very appreciative of the interest taken in it by the audience, were more than pleased by the evident pleasure and enjoyment the audience got out of the operetta, and ended the program by having the audience join them in singing "Oh Come All Ye Faithful."

As the last strains of the song died away, Santa Claus suddenly appeared on the stage, greeted all the boys and girls as they crowded 'round, and greeted a great group who had come in from the rear entrance just at the close of the program. Treats were handed out, of course, and every one went home feeling that the Chester schools had again demonstrated their ability to put on a good program when the need arises.

Chester Liberty County Times,
December 26, 1957

Moore Christmas Tree, 1958

In many of Montana's smaller communities, the 1950s provided an opportunity for the resurrection of earlier traditions suspended by the Depression and

World War II. Such was the case in Moore—a small ranching settlement about fifteen miles southwest of Lewistown, in Fergus County—where the community Christmas tree reappeared in 1958.

*I*N SPITE OF HEAVY SNOWS, storms, and bad roads, the Christmas tree for Moore was made a reality this year when it was placed on the band stand on Main Street.

Strung with lights, glowing with color every evening, it shines a welcome, and a message of "Merry Christmas" to all, as well as a reminder of "Peace on Earth, Good Will to Men."

Town officials responded to the entreaties of the members of the Moore Woman's Club for the tree, and did all the erecting and lighting for the community. Credit for getting the tree goes to Mayor Elbert Larson, with the assistance of Wayne Hannah, who took his jeep to go way back into the mountains to get this extra large tree, and bring it down, in spite of the snow.

It reminds early-day residents of the days when Moore used to observe Christmas with the erecting of a tree at this time of the year. One of the first large trees was brought down by Ross Brown who, back in 1915, was manager of the old Harlow ranch up Rock Creek. The snow was not so bad that year, and the tree secured was unusually large. It took a four-horse team to do the job, tall ladders, and a lot of men to make it stand in its majesty in the center of the town square.

Lewistown Daily News, December 21, 1958

Lewistown Christmas Shopping, 1958

The post–World War II period brought prosperity in varying degrees to most Montanans. The state's businessmen focused on the Christmas buying season, and it quickly became the major component of their annual retail sales. In Lewistown, situated in the middle of the state, a report on 1958 Christmas sales hints at the spirit of economic optimism that pervades a state where long-term economic stability has been elusive.

$\mathcal{C}$HRISTMAS SHOPPING in Lewistown zoomed towards its climactic three days and possible seasonal sales records Saturday with most stores jammed with customers almost until the 9 p.m. closing hour.

Business owners around town reported extra-heavy seasonal business, and anticipated possible record sales this year.

Stores, also slated to stay open until 9 p.m. Monday, were heavily crowded during the Saturday rush hours, and even heavier shopping in the final three days was predicted.

Most local business observers credited hazardous road conditions and an intensified "Buy at Home" campaign for the heavy business.

One store owner said, "We're doing more business now than I can ever remember having had on this or any other occasion."

Lewistown Daily News, December 21, 1958

Crow Indian Christmas, 1958

Because the holiday of Christmas was brought to Montana by whites, many of the state's Native Americans assumed some of the Yuletide traditions only gradually. At the Baptist Mission—situated in Lodge Grass, on the Crow Reservation—the Christmas pageant has become a local tradition.

$\mathcal{A}$T THE TURN of the century, the Crow Indians knew very little of Christmas or Jesus Christ, but they did know a Jesus Man by the name of the Rev. W. A. Petzoldt.

In 1903, the Crows began to learn more of Christmas and of the significance of Christ's birth. That year on Christmas, the Crows had gathered in a tent and, after hearing the story of the birth of our Lord, given by Dr. Petzoldt, they had a feast, seated on the ground. This became the custom for the next several years, until the first Crow Indian Baptist Mission was built.

Mrs. Petzoldt felt that the uneducated Indians would have a better understanding and a keener appreciation of the significance of Christ's birth through the medium of pageantry. Thus was born the Crow Indian pageant, which has become an annual presentation for all the Crow Indian Reservation.

Each year, the pageant has become bigger and better. The people began to have a better understanding and a deeper feeling for the story of the Christ Child and the joy and good will that are revealed by it. Mrs. Petzoldt made a special study of Christmas pictures so that the costumes and scenes would be not only authentic but beautifully artistic.

Each year changes were made in order to achieve those ideas. As Christmas draws near, the people look forward to playing their part in telling the greatest story every known to mankind.

Agnes Deernose played the part of Mary for 20 years, and three years ago her daughter, Ferole Pease, took this part.

George Pease, Sr., has always been in charge of the stage and lighting effects.

Grandma Sarah Pease made a realistic looking lamb which the littlest shepherd boy always carried. It was a tradition that a little boy from a faithful church family would have the role until he outgrew the part.

This year Mrs. H. S. Benson will direct the choir. Mrs. Petzoldt directed the choir until three years ago, when ill health prevented her from doing the work. The Rev. Herschell Daney, pastor of the Baptist Mission, will direct the pageant this year.

John White Man Runs Him has always played the part of one of the wise men, not only in the pageant, but in real life, according to the pastor.

"John is one of the millions that are wise men, bringing gold and frankincense, and myrrh to God. In every country, near and far, wise men and women see Jesus as the light of the world and try to follow Him. We bring gold and frankincense and myrrh, like the wise men of old.

"We have books and money, which represent gold. Whenever we give food to hungry people, or clothing to those who are shivering with cold, whenever we give money to help doctors deal with the sick, and teachers to educate the ignorant, and pastors to guide them in God's ways, we are giving gold to Jesus," the director said.

This annual Christmas pageant will be presented at the First Crow Indian Baptist Church in Lodge Grass, Sunday, December 21, beginning at 8 p.m.

Hardin Tribune-Herald, December 18, 1958

Hardin Christmas Tradition, 1959

In many smaller Montana towns during the twentieth century, Christmas traditions developed because of the work of one or two selfless individuals. In Hardin, for example, the annual Christmas program at the Harriet Theatre spanned decades, to the delight of generations of local children.

*V*ERA WHEELER can claim quite a record—24 consecutive years of Christmas shows for the kids at the Harriet Theatre. And her parents before her had given this treat to Hardin youngsters. There are many children going to the Christmas shows now whose parents before them enjoyed the hospitality of the Harriet.

But did you ever stop to think that this is a treat for busy parents as well as for children? And it works for the benefit of other business people, too. Mom and Dad can get a lot more shopping done while Homer and Vera are "babysitting" than they could if the kids all trailed along.

The Wheelers tell me that approximately 1,000 kids were jammed into the Theatre—which seats something over 600.

Hardin Tribune-Herald, December 24, 1959

Lodge Grass Christmas Happenings, 1959

The town of Lodge Grass is located in Big Horn County, on the eastern portion of the Crow Indian Reservation. In a short piece by the town's local correspondent, the traditional Montana Christmas focus on church and school is evident.

*T*HE JUNIOR-HIGH Sunday School class of the Little Brown Church decorated the Christmas tree on Friday evening after school. Following their work, they enjoyed a hamburger fry in the church basement.

The girls of the Future Home Makers unit in Lodge Grass High School enjoyed a Christmas party on the evening of December 14. The evening began with caroling around town. Later the girls made hot chocolate at the home economics room at school. They also made candy and pop-corn balls for a needy family in town.

Hardin Tribune-Herald, December 24, 1959

Christmas Television in Miles City, 1962

The availability of commercial television became relatively widespread in Montana during the 1960s. Although some charged that the state's particular brand of culture would be homogenized into a bland national character by the invasion of television, most Montanans embraced this technological advance. In 1962, the Miles City newspaper assessed the television fare for that Christmas season.

*T*HE CHRISTMAS COMMERCIAL, which started with gift themes on Halloween—or so it seemed—disappeared at midnight Monday as if a magic eraser had moved over the television screens.

The holiday, for many the end of a four-day weekend, was obviously considered to be less than ideal for relaxed, concentrated viewing. Tuesday, although the regular daytime shows tried to compete with family talk and unwrapping gifts in millions of living rooms, many of the performers acted as if they didn't believe they had very large or attentive audiences. Some local news shows, without much news to report, introduced behind-the-camera helpers. Even the weather girls made their reports in leisurely manners.

The most impressive Christmas television was the religious services. Watching a church service through the miracle of television is not the same thing as going to church, but the midnight services were impressive. Millions could see cathedrals that they may never visit in person.

Bing Crosby seemed subdued and almost uncomfortable in his Christmas Eve special on ABC. Costar Mary Martin, an energetic performer, appeared to be carrying the major burden in the low-key show.

It was rather disappointing—bits and pieces of music and talk, and none of it too engaging. Highlight was the singing of the United Nations Children's Choir—cute children of U.N. personnel.

It was ABC's initial dip into color television and the producers appeared a little frightened and tentative about it. . . .

Miles City Star, December 26, 1962

Community Christmas in Wagner, 1963

The town of Wagner is located on the Milk River in Phillips County, about ten miles west of Malta. As its correspondent to the Malta weekly newspaper notes, this community continued into the 1960s to celebrate Christmas in small ways—each steeped in local tradition.

*T*HE FRIENDLY NEIGHBORS CLUB held its annual Christmas party recently at the South Wagner School, with 22 members and two visitors present. Entertainment for the afternoon was provided by the school children singing several songs, accompanied by their teacher, Mrs. Cookingham. The ladies sang "Silent Night" and "Jingle Bells," and there were several Christmas readings.

The tables were decorated in the Christmas theme. Each member had favors and a gift hankie from the Club. Gifts were exchanged and "secret pals" revealed. "Secret pal" names were drawn again for next year. Each member brought some of her favorite homemade candy, and sandwiches, pickles, and coffee were served. Santa arrived at the very end with gifts for the members and for all of the small children. . . .

Malta Phillips County News, December 26, 1963

Highwood Christmas News, 1963

Highwood is a small ranching community about twenty-five miles east of Great Falls, in Chouteau County. A summary of the town's Christmas activities in 1963 reveals a mixture of some very traditional activities with some long-distance traveling. In this setting, the emphases on simple acts of giving and family reunions are evident.

THE FIFTH- AND SIXTH-GRADE Sunday School class of the Methodist Church, with their teachers, Mrs. Don Huffman and Mrs. Conn Forder, were out singing carols around town on Monday evening. The Methodist Youth Fellowship and the CYC young folks were also singing Christmas carols on Wednesday evening. Both groups had refreshments at the Church after caroling. The songs were all enjoyed at the homes they visited.

Mr. and Mrs. Lee Phillips of Minneapolis arrived by train this weekend to visit their respective parents, the Hardee Phillips' and the Fred Woodmanseys', for the holidays. Lee attends the University of Minnesota, and Jane teaches in one of the Minneapolis schools.

Mrs. Myrtle Davison is leaving on Thursday to fly to San Diego, California, to visit her son Bob and his family, and her daughters Irene and Marjorie and their families, who live in Fresno. The trip was Bob's Christmas present to his mother.

Sandra White left Friday for Darby, Montana, to spend the holidays at her home there. Mrs. Rae Keaster is teaching in her place. Dixie Golden is leaving Monday for her home in Kevin for the holidays. Lila Pasha will be teaching in her place.

Fort Benton River Press, December 25, 1963

Christmas Tree Customs, 1963

The Christmas-tree industry in Montana, which dates to the 1920s, had developed into a significant seasonal business by the 1960s. Like other symbols of the holidays, this traditional item suffers the whims of popular fashion.

THE OLD family Christmas tree ain't what it used to be, or words to that effect. American Christmas-tree shoppers have gone from spruce to Balsam to Douglas fir to pine. And, in recent years, a fellow with a sheet of aluminum and a tin snips has given the tree growers something to worry about.

According to George Blake, assistant professor of forestry at Montana State University, the end in style changes of Christmas trees is not yet in sight. One of the most recent developments is the "shaped" tree, a tree that has undergone careful trimming and shaping during its years of growth until it looks like something out of a decorative planting by the time it's ready for market.

The Montana harvest of trees for the holidays was pretty well over before Thanksgiving, Blake said. One thing about the harvest that some people are now aware of is that many of the trees this year started out to be limbs. In a cutting process called "stump culture," a Douglas fir is lopped off with a branch or two remaining on the stump. One of these branches then becomes a leader and the tree grows a new top, ready for another harvest in from five to 15 years.

Blake said that Christmas-tree farms near some of the larger cities have started the practice of urging people to come out and cut their own tree, somewhat in the ancient spirit of bringing in the yule log.

"Only angle the Christmas tree merchants haven't figured out yet is what to do with a tree on the day after Christmas, short of putting it in a nice big bonfire," Blake said. *Malta Phillips County News*, December 26, 1963

Fort Benton Kiwanis Christmas Party, 1963

As growing numbers of young people leave Montana's smaller communities in search of higher education or employment, one holiday phenomenon has been their annual return to spend Christmas with their family and friends. In Fort Benton (an agricultural community located on the Missouri River, about 40 miles northeast of Great Falls), a local service club turned this phenomenon into an annual tradition.

COLLEGE STUDENTS and service personnel home for the holidays have been invited to the annual Kiwanis entertainment, to be held this Saturday night at 6:30 in the IOOF Hall. The homecoming young people will be guests of the club.

Hugh Simmons, Fort Benton superintendent, reports sending 88 invitations to those known to be either at college or in service. Should any have been missed, they are urged to contact him or Ray Bennett not later than Saturday morning, to permit advance planning for an expected capacity crowd.

The annual entertainment provides an ideal get-together for many vacationing young people.

The list provided shows that a big majority, 34 of 41, of last year's graduates are attending college or in service. There were 23 from the class of 1962, 19 of the 1961 graduates in institutions of higher education or in service, and twelve from earlier years. Some may have been missed, of course, which is the reason for asking such to contact the sponsors and arrange to come.

Fort Benton River Press, December 25, 1963

Christmas for Missile Guardians, 1964

One of the roles Montana played in the post–World War II Cold War was the situation, within her borders, of Minuteman Missile silos. While most Montanans celebrated a traditional Christmas Day across the state in 1964, some Air Force personnel spent the day deep underground.

CHRISTMAS WILL BE just another working day for the men who will launch America's Minuteman Missiles should be nation be plunged into nuclear war.

They will put in their regular 12-hour duty tours in underground launch control centers scattered across a vast area of central Montana from which 150 pre-aimed missiles could start flying toward enemy targets moments after the President gave the word.

These highly trained Air Force officers are on constant alert, two in each of the 15 centers where they monitor electronically—and fire, if necessary—the missiles in unmanned underground silos.

Once they are in the reinforced concrete capsule buried 80 feet in the ground, they can't leave until their 12 hours are up.

Christmas dinner will be taken to them by elevator from a service building on the surface, which contains a kitchen, dining room, recreation room, security office, and sleeping quarters for the security guards and cooks, as well as occasional maintenance people.

Billings Gazette, December 25, 1964

A Vietnam Christmas, 1965

The war in Vietnam had escalated during the early 1960s. By 1965 the United States had almost 200,000 military personnel in that country—and would station more than 500,000 Americans there by the end of the decade. As U.S. troop commitments rose, so did opposition on the home front to U.S. involvement in Southeast Asia. On the occasion of Christmas 1965, an editor of the *Billings Gazette* wrestled with the inconsistencies of warfare and the holiday message of peace.

Carter soldier Lones Wigger, Jr., kneeling with Vietnamese child. Montana Historical Society Photograph Archives, Helena

*N*EITHER SILENT nor holy is Christmas in this land of war. There is no calm, no peace.

But is it so different than it has always been? Even that year, when a Prince of Peace was born into a kingdom of combat, there was torment and suffering over the land.

It has always been thus. At Jerusalem, at Gettysburg, at Flanders, at Bataan. At the Ia Drang Valley in Viet Nam. And almost apologetically men celebrate, each time, the birth of One who, above all others, loathed man's destruction of himself.

Man's hope, of course, will be reflected by a star in the East here this Christmas, but it will be fogged by the smoke of battle. And that is the irony: that each man here will have no other light to guide him but dim lessons mislearned in history.

He, that figure of any man in khaki, wrapped in heavy gear, no brightness anywhere about him but the light of his eyes. His face lined. His shoulders weighted. His step slow and disciplined.

Yes, always thus. At Valley Forge, at Normandy, at Pork Chop Hill. And at Plei Me, Viet Nam.

Devout man shrinks from accepting the responsibility of war. But he accepts the responsibility of improving it.

Battles, in this age, are transacted by machines ever more perfect. We move faster, hit harder. We advance destruction artificially. But we die as before and grieve as men have always grieved.

And those who live, perhaps, suffer the supreme agony. They, here this Christmas, are apart from their people. And although one can protect himself from flak in a foxhole, loneliness penetrates all armor. Separation wounds all.

Christmas, 1965—12,000 miles from home, will be neither silent nor holy. Man is a slave to his rifle.

But still he believes, he hopes. He bows his head this Christmas and asks that his cause be just.

Billings Gazette, December 25, 1965

Roundup Church Open House, 1965

The charge that "Christmas has become too commercial" carries a long history in America. That assertion gained particular prominence in Montana during the 1960s, when many residents shared in the growing national affluence. In Roundup—the county seat of Musselshell County, located about 50 miles north of Billings—one minister's answer to that charged proved especially inspired.

*C*HRISTMAS DAY between the hours of 3:00 and 6:00, the sanctuary of St. Paul's Lutheran Church, 1009 First Street West will become an "open house" for any who wish to concentrate on the true meaning of Christmas— the blessing of the Savior's birth.

The church will be decorated especially for the occasion. No formal service will be held. Individuals or families will be able to make a special journey to the manger for their brief meditation. Ushers will allow one family or individual to proceed up the aisle at a time in order to avoid a rushed atmosphere.

Commenting on the "Journey to Bethlehem," Pastor Lowell Siebrass had this to say: "Christmas has become so commercialized and man-centered we often forget whose birthday it is. This is an opportunity we offer people of our community to take time out in the rushed season for a few quiet moments of prayer and meditation before the Christ Child of Bethlehem.

"Every year at Christmastide thousands of dedicated Christians make a special pilgrimage to the Church of the Nativity in Bethlehem, but this is a privilege few of us will ever experience. Still there are so many who wish to take a few quiet moments with their families for private worship.

This is now the second year we have staged the 'Journey to Bethlehem.' We were persuaded by the comments last year to have it again. Families who made the 'Journey' before indicate that this was one of the most meaningful worship experiences they had ever known, especially for the children. We hope more and more people will avail themselves of this opportunity."

Roundup Record-Tribune, December 23, 1965

Billings Neighborhood Contribution, 1965

One of the more inspiring aspects of Christmas—in Montana and throughout the Christian world—is the way in which individuals and small groups take on holiday projects that become local traditions. Just such a case involves the Gregory Hills subdivision in Billings in 1965.

*N*ESTLED UNDER an overhanging rock—250 feet above Billings— stands a 40-foot symbol of a neighborhood's collective imagination . . . a decorated Christmas tree.

The decorated lodgepole pine growing about halfway up the Rimrocks overlooks Gregory Hills subdivision, north of Rimrock Road on Billings' west end.

At night, under a mantle of 650 colored Christmas lights, it is not hard to spot.

Decorating the stately pine tree originated with Mr. and Mrs. James Reger, 3139 Gregory Lane.

Mrs. Reger got the ball rolling early in December by making telephone

Governor Tim Babcock (seated right) hosting a Christmas luncheon on December 23, 1965. Chet Dreher, photographer, Montana Historical Society Photograph Archives, Helena

calls to each of the other 14 families in the subdivision, as well as to R. A. Mikelson, 3004 Radcliffe Drive, the Gregory Hills developer and contractor, asking for volunteers.

She met with resounding success.

The entire neighborhood wanted to help, as did four families whose homes aren't even finished yet.

Early Saturday, December 11, the assault on the selected tree began. Nearly every family turned out en masse to help—each with at least one string of tree lights.

Battling chilly weather and a stiff wind, the tree was remodeled from a well-weathered veteran of Montana winters to a shining example of what a determined neighborhood can do.

The decorators utilized ladders, poles, and children to complete the feat.

Two of the Regers' boys, Randy, 15, and Steve, 12, shinnied up the tree to place lights on the top.

Two 16-foot aluminum poles bound together aided workers in draping the rest of 25 strings of lights on the wide branches. And ladders braced against the cliffside assisted helpers on the ground.

A Billings electrical firm solved the power-supply problem. They donated and installed a 550-foot conduit cable, connected with a 70-amp circuit breaker, from the tree to the Reger home at the base of the rims.

"We'll all chip in if the power bill runs too high," Mikelson said when questioned about the increased use of electricity in the Reger home.

One motive for the gigantic tree—which Gregory Hills residents claim to be the tallest decorated tree in Billings—is the lack of trees on lawns of homes.

The trees down below are only a year old. The subdivision is just over four years old.

"And this is just the beginning," residents proudly proclaim. "We're going to make this a yearly custom, and improve on it each year," one woman declared.

"Neighborhood children enjoy the tree, too. The day after it was decorated, about 30 of them climbed the trail and had a 'Christmas Carol Concert' under the tree's limbs."

They planned to do it again Christmas Eve. And next year . . . and the next.

Billings Gazette, December 24, 1965

Holiday Decorating Tips from Thompson Falls, 1967

No one ever accused Montanans of failing to be inventive and adaptive during the Christmas season. A case in point is Bill Chisenhall, a barber in Thompson Falls.

$\mathcal{B}$ILL CHISENHALL runs a barber shop in Thompson Falls. Obtaining a Christmas tree to use in decorating his shop for the yule season presents no problem to him. He simply loads his corner Dieffenbachia plant with cones, icicles, lights, and elves. He even places a Nativity scene at the bottom. Bill fell heir to the plant about four years ago, when it grew too tall for the mobile home of his mother-in-law, Mrs. Gordon Shoemaker. The tree is now nearly eight feet tall.

Thompson Falls Sanders County Ledger, December 21, 1967

Christmas Aid for Butte, 1967

The Christmas of 1967 was seriously muted in Butte and Anaconda because of a months-long strike against the area's major employer, the Anaconda Copper Mining Company. A ripple effect ran through the state's entire economy and reached into other Montana towns. In the spirit of the holidays, however, the strikers' families received some assistance just prior to Christmas Day.

*C*HRISTMAS CHEER for families of members of Butte Miners Union No. 1 and Anaconda Local 6002 has been received—11 tons of it.

Union members and residents of Yellowstone County, and people from Park, Stillwater, and Carbon Counties provided the pre-Christmas lift last Saturday.

Received at the Miners Union Hall were 13,000 pounds of potatoes, two tons of dried beans, three tons of canned goods, and a wide variety of clothing and toys.

One-half of the contributions went to the Butte Miners Union, and the other half to the Anaconda local.

The estimated 6,000 miners and their families in the Butte-Anaconda area have been idled for nearly six months by the strike; no negotiations in Montana, at least, have been scheduled.

Missoula Missoulian, December 25, 1967

Missoula Christmas Workers, 1967

As the excitement, the rush, and the demands of Christmas build each year, we tend to forget that some Montanans are not able to share the traditional

Christmas activities. In 1967 Missoulians were reminded of those people whose Christmas was altered by necessity.

*W*HILE YOU'RE EATING that holiday turkey and watching the football games on TV, or playing with your son's new electric train, or just loafing around the house Christmas Day, it might be well to remember that thousands of people around the country will have to postpone their hours of relaxation and celebration until they have put in their time at the job on that special holiday.

When you are waking from that "long winter's nap," night watchmen are just getting in, and before they partake of their children's delight, will sleep.

When you are returning home after offering worship in church, the young lad who delivered this newspaper to your door is just getting in from his route.

About the time you switch on your television for the day's sports programs, police officers are taking time out for a quick lunch at home or at the local café.

Nurses, firemen, deputies, highway patrolmen, railroad workers, bus drivers, taxi drivers, newspapermen, ambulance drivers, weathermen, airline hostesses, pilots, and our servicemen around the globe, will be devoting long hours of their time in seeing to it that you and I are able to spend a relaxed Christmas with our families and loved ones.

And lest I forget, the jolly ole man himself will be spending a lot of his time climbing up and down chimneys, unloading toys, and feeding his reindeer. Yes, even Santa Claus will have to work on Christmas.

Missoula Missoulian, December 24, 1967

Thompson Falls Decorates for Christmas, 1967

The annual practice of municipal decorations in a town's business district has been widespread in Montana. In Thompson Falls, that tradition dates to 1949 when the trees themselves were moved into place. Particularly in smaller Montana communities, the responsibility for the municipal decorating long has been assumed by civic groups.

$\mathcal{T}$HE LIGHTS ON THE spruce trees along the north side of Main Street went up for the 18th yule season Saturday with members of the Thompson Falls Lions Club and employees of the Montana Power Company and Mountain States Telephone doing the work.

On hand for their 18th year were two Lions—M. C. Sutherland and Harold Jensen—who were members of the original crew moving the trees in the winter of 1949 from the court house.

Sutherland said that holes about 10 feet by 10 feet and four to five feet deep were dug before the frost settled and the ground was also dug out around the trees and wire netting placed around the root bases. Then a large steel pan or skid was slid under the root ball and the trees were pulled to their new home. The 16 trees average about 12 feet in height. Each with its ball of dirt is believed to have weighed up to about a ton.

The actual moving of the trees was done in January. Only one tree failed to survive, but at the time, Sutherland and Jensen recall there were many "doubting Thomases" in the city and a few who made bets that were never paid or collected.

In the ensuing years, the Lions and the Business and Professional Women purchased lights to decorate the trees.

Thompson Falls Sanders County Ledger, December 7, 1967

Santa Visits West Yellowstone, 1968

As its name implies, West Yellowstone is located at the west entrance to Yellowstone National Park, in southernmost Gallatin County, at an elevation of more than 6,600 feet. The community's Christmas activities necessarily are adapted to its unusual winter environment.

$\mathcal{F}$OR NEARLY ALL CHILDREN across the nation, Christmas Eve is the time that Santa Claus and his reindeer pay them a visit. But for this small mountain community nestled in the Rocky Mountains, the afternoon before Christmas is when he arrives.

Tradition has it that Santa Claus always comes to West Yellowstone first because West Yellowstone is the closest thing in the country to the North Pole.

Oldtimers, who have lived in the area since the town's conception in 1908, say Santa always comes in the early afternoon, either by horse-drawn sleigh or dog sled, with gifts for the town's young children.

Modern times have caught up with the jolly old elf, however, as he now arrives by snowmobile, pulling his sleigh full of goodies behind him.

The lack of reindeer has been accepted by the town's children with the explanation that they are "resting" before their night's work.

Castle Geyser in action, Yellowstone National Park, 1887. F. Jay Haynes, photographer, Haynes Foundation Collection, Montana Historical Society Photograph Archives, Helena

Snow is no problem at this entrance to the nation's first national park. There is roughly three feet on the ground now, and by mid-January, it will be about six feet deep.

The average winter's snowfall is about 25 feet, but fortunately it doesn't all remain.

Great Falls Tribune, December 24, 1969

Tribune Christmas Wishes, 1969

At the end of the turbulent decade of the 1960s, the editors of the *Great Falls Tribune* took the opportunity of the Christmas Day edition to make some pertinent Yuletide wishes for the state of Montana.

*I*F WE HAD A magic lantern and a responsive genie to carry out our own Christmas wishes for Montana, we would seek:

An end to the disastrous war in Vietnam, which has cost the lives of 204 Montana young men.

An end to the horrible carnage on the highways, which recorded 330 fatalities as of Wednesday.

An aggressive start to end the pollution of our air and waters.

A program to use our magnificent natural resources in the best possible manner—remembering that this generation has a deep obligation to future generations to be responsible stewards of this land and resources that previous generations passed on to us.

Great Falls Tribune, December 25, 1969

Great Falls Christmas Shopping, 1969

Despite some irregular harvests that locally affected stockmen and farmers, most Montanans shared in the national prosperity of the 1960s. They were bolstered by petroleum and strippable-coal booms, and by the general growth of the tourist industry. That widespread condition is reflected in a report of Christmas-shopping trends in Great Falls at the end of the decade.

*I*T'S CHRISTMAS as usual—and in some cases a little better, according to the managers of some of Great Falls' larger stores.

At the Paris, sales are up over last year, although customers have informed sales people that they won't be spending as much this year on larger items. Regardless of what customers say, however, at the Paris, such items as televisions and the household goods are going well.

One trend that has been noted at the Paris is a preference among many customers for practical gifts. A new gourmet shop is attracting Christmas buyers with unusual gifts for the home, but standby electrical appliances and other household items also are selling well.

At Sears, sales are reported about the same as last year, but the last-minute rush seems bigger this year.

Sears customers are buying everything, the manager said, but color televisions, pool tables, dishwashers, and small appliances are going especially well.

Sales at Buttrey's downtown store are somewhat down this year, because of the opening of the suburban store, according to the manager. There's a big Christmas last-minute rush this year, he said, and sales over-all are beyond expectations in all departments.

Penney's manager also termed business this year "about the same." He also noted a last-minute rush that he suspects is because of unusually good pre-Christmas weather.

At Penney's the more expensive items are also moving more slowly this year, although customers seem to be buying more smaller items to make up for a big one.

The manager of Montgomery Wards, where business is ahead this year, said that unlike other reports, large items are going well. The stereo-tape field is very big this year, he said, for both automobiles and the home. In fact, he added, all of the equipment in the home-entertainment field is going exceptionally well.

At Valu-Mart, sales are up 20 per cent this year, the manager reported. He said that major-appliance sales are up a whopping 74 per cent, and the camera department is well over last year's sales too. He also disagreed with the idea that expensive gifts are not going as well.

Among the most popular gifts being sold at Valu-Mart, he said, are blenders, electric hairsetters, tape recorders, mother's rings, pool tables, and portable organs. Good weather has hurt two departments, automotive and shoes, where snow tires and snow boots are having a bad year.

Great Falls Tribune, December 24, 1969

Montana and the New West

ECENT MONTANA is characterized by a strong environmental movement in the 1970s, a new state Constitution in 1972, a drop in population during the 1980s, and a dramatic rise in immigration to the state in the 1990s. Montana politics became more conservative during the era, and voters sent the first Republican to the U.S. Senate since 1946.

Montana's economy shifted wildly during the last three decades of the twentieth century. An evolution from traditional natural-resource extraction to a tourism and service-based economy triggered falling per-capita incomes and job dislocation. The demise of the "Montana Twins"—the Anaconda Company and the Montana Power Company—symbolized this radical change. Montanans reacted by celebrating Christmas with greater fervor, at ever-increasing expense.

However—as has been the case for almost two hundred years—Christmas is what we make it. We can make it sacred and peaceful. We can make it hectic and frantic. We can make it an opportunity to share with those less fortunate. We can make it solely commercial. We can make it simple and joyous. *We* determine our traditions. The decision merits our thought and attention.

Merry Christmas!

Montana's excellent downhill skiing has long attracted Christmas vacationers to Big Sky Country. Montana Historical Society Photograph Archives, Helena

Livingston Christmas Observations, 1970

In 1970 the Northern Pacific Railroad was still the prime employer in the town of Livingston, the county seat of Park County. Within a year the Burlington Northern merger would become a reality, and this railroad town would begin a series of economic and social adjustments. In this context, the editor of the *Livingston Enterprise* wrote a holiday editorial that emphasizes the essence of Christmas.

$\mathcal{E}$VERY SEASON, each holiday of the year brings some kind of change into the pattern of our lives. But, of all the days, in summer, winter, spring, or fall, there is—for everyone—a most favorite of all.

It is, of course, the Christmas.

We are captured by the spirit of Christmas long before the holiday arrives. The commercial aspects, the bright streets, decorated windows, and well-stocked store shelves—these are obvious witness to the fact that Christ-

Christmas card from the Montana Stockgrowers Association with drawing by Mons Teigen, 1969. Montana Historical Society Museum, Helena

mas is soon coming. But, the real change is something that takes place within the heart and the spirit. It touches first the very young. It comes to the school scene. It reaches out to the older community. Some grasp it eagerly; a few, reluctantly. But even the most persistent die-hard eventually becomes captive to the mood, throws away a year-around frown, walks with a sprightly step, and offers a merry greeting to all the world.

As the holiday grows nearer, the spirit of warmth and happiness brings to each individual opportunity to share in the most magnificent moment of all time—the birth of Jesus Christ, the Redeemer. This is the essence, the origin of anticipation—the realization that God sent his only son into the world.

Livingston Enterprise, December 24, 1970

Ashland Family Christmas, 1971

Ashland is a small ranching community in Rosebud County, just to the east of the Northern Cheyenne Indian Reservation and close to the heart of the strippable-coal country. In 1971 the Ashland correspondent to the *Powder River Examiner* in Broadus was Cynda Dodge. She took the opportunity of her Christmas column to describe her family's Christmas preparations. In recounting these holiday activities, Mrs. Dodge gives some real insight into the celebration of a rural Montana Christmas.

SUNDAY WAS A BEAUTIFUL DAY, with the sun shining brightly, so Jim and Kelly went forth to cut our Christmas tree. My spouse claims I am pretty fussy about my tree, but he has always complied and scoured the hills for one that is just right. This year he and Kelly came in with a lovely juniper that he had to trim down to fit between the floor and the ceiling. His part done, Jim turned it over to the family for decorating.

Seeing the tree anew, through the eyes of our little ones, brings back memories of Christmases long ago, when I was tortured by the wait for the morning when I would get up to find that Santa Claus had finally made his visit. How slow that day was in coming! (Well, I'm not all *that* old, but it's been awhile!)

This year I will again be reliving my childhood through Kelly and Alan: writing a list for Santa and leaving it under the tree, fixing him a snack, and putting out carrots or sugar for the reindeer who work so hard delivering all those toys. Perhaps that is one of the reasons Santa has lived to such a ripe old age. We relish feeling those joyous days and beliefs come to life again, through our own children.

Broadus Powder River Examiner, December 23, 1971

Broadus Senior Citizens Hold Party, 1971

With the proliferation of senior-citizen centers and retirement homes in post–World War II Montana, new arenas were created in which Christmas could be celebrated. At a senior-citizen center in Broadus, activities were lively in 1971.

*T*HE BROADUS SENIOR CITIZENS met December 16th at the Center for a no-host Christmas party. There were 32 in attendance. Everyone especially enjoyed the decorated tree awaiting them—thanks to the Rainbow Girls and the Pink Panther 4-H Club.

Gift exchange, an abundance of "goodies," and singing of Christmas carols made it a very festive party. Cards were signed and sent to absent members. Thanks were expressed to the Lutheran Ladies for the nice party enjoyed at their Fellowship Room on December 14th.

Broadus Powder River Examiner, December 23,1971

Napi Creates Christmas on the Blackfeet Reservation

In 1972 the Christmas program at the Starr School on the Blackfeet Indian Reservation was a remarkable production. For this occasion, Miss Tia White Grass, the school's Head Start and kindergarten aide, wrote and narrated a drama presented by the students. Her work, titled "What Happened When Napi

Made Christmas," considers the issue of Native Americans and the initially white holiday of Christmas.

𝒥N THE OLD DAYS, before the white man came to this land, the Blackfeet did not celebrate Christmas. In fact, it wasn't until recent years that Indians celebrated this holiday as the white men do. But, when people turned toward Christianity, they started rejoicing the birth of Christ as the white people do now. The Christmas was usually celebrated by having a big dance, feasting with friends, and exchanging gifts.

In the Blackfeet legend, Napi created this world and the people in it. But nowhere in the memory of the old ones or in any story is there any mention of Napi creating Christmas. So the following story was written contemplating what might have happened if Napi did make the Indian Christmas:

Once long ago, Napi and his people were in their winter camp along the Two Medicine River. It was during the Moon of Cold Weather or December. On this particular morning, Napi woke up and was very surprised to see the sun shining so brightly. It was very unusual because he could hear the birds singing, as if they were calling out for everyone to get up and enjoy the day.

When Napi stepped out of his lodge, he was surprised indeed. For here was a day that was as warm and beautiful as any day in the spring. This was very strange because it was in the middle of winter and here was a day like spring. But this made Napi very happy. He felt so good, he decided that he and his people should celebrate the day. So he went around telling everyone to prepare for a big celebration, for there would be much feasting and dancing.

While the people were getting things ready, Napi realized that something was missing. Then he called his people together again and told them that they should invite their brothers and sisters from the mountains and prairies to come and share in their good time.

So he sent some young boys out to invite all the animals he could find. First the boys found some deer in the forest and, as they went along, they met a wolf. Then they found some birds, and invited them. Then they came down onto the prairie, where they told all the buffalo to come and help celebrate this special day.

Forrest DeRosia and his dog team, Libby, 1913. Montana Historical Society Photograph Archives, Helena

The boys brought back into camp as many animal brothers and sisters as they could find. There the people met them and made them feel welcome. All the people and animals were happy, and much feasting and visiting went on through the day. Towards evening the head buffalo asked everyone to listen to what he had to say. When all grew silent, he spoke. "I have enjoyed myself so much today, I wish to give my people brothers and sisters a gift. Since you have no fur of your own, I give you mine so you will always be warm." This gift was received gratefully.

Then the wolf rose to speak. "I am also happy and I wish to give you something. I give you my knowledge and cunning. With this you will become great hunters and never go hungry." This made the people happy.

Then the deer spoke. "I give you something that is different. I give you my hooves, so you can make pretty noises as you dance." The young braves were especially glad for this.

Last, the birds spoke. "All we have to give you are our feathers. But take them and make yourselves just as pretty as the noises around your ankles."

All these gifts were so great and they gave the people such a good feeling, they felt that they should also give the animals something. One of the chiefs stood and spoke for the people. He told the animals that since they had given them such great gifts there was only one thing the people could give in return that would be equal. . . .

"We give you our songs and dances. That way you will always have a way to show how happy you are. And you will also know that good feeling of sharing with others."

The animals were overjoyed. For this is the one thing their people brothers and sisters had that they, the animals, envied.

So animals and people alike were so pleased they joined together to sing and dance and celebrate all night long.

Maybe this is why Napi did not make a Christmas for the Indians. Because giving and receiving gifts and sharing with others was something that happened every day—not just something you waited to do on special holidays.

Browning Glacier Reporter, December 28, 1972

Livingston Christmas Rush, 1972

In the decades following World War II, the development of Christmas as a major commercial enterprise escalated dramatically. Nowhere was this trend more apparent than in the post offices of Montana communities. Not all of the state's postal operations were as successful as that of Livingston in 1972.

A WEEK AGO at this time, Postmaster Wally Paterson was worried that he and his busy crew would be unable to "wade through" the huge volume of Christmas mail at the post office.

"Things look much brighter now," the postmaster said Thursday.

"Monday, December 18, appeared to have been the 'crossroads' day for incoming and outgoing mail volumes.

"We were fortunate in being able to secure two new experienced employees, Jack Bristol and Dale Gardner, just in time for the Christmas rush. Bristol transferred here from Florida and Gardner is a transfer from Illinois.

"We are still short on help but with the co-operation of our customers in mailing earlier, the flow of Christmas mail was heavy but seemed to be more even; the crew was able to process it and keep it moving.

"This holiday season we were able to secure additional truck transportation from the Billings Sectional Center whenever mail volumes were excessive.

"With good luck and good weather, we will wind up the Christmas season at 5:30 p.m. Friday with all Christmas mail delivered. The post office windows will be closed Sunday and Monday, giving our employees a well-deserved long holiday weekend."

A window will be open Saturday at the post office for delivery of "will call" packages and parcels, Paterson said.

Livingston Enterprise, December 21, 1972

Circle Christmas Program, 1973

The public-school building long has been the site of the annual Christmas presentation in many Montana communities. In Circle, that tradition was continued with a Christmas program in 1973.

A CHRISTMAS PROGRAM sponsored by the Speech Class of Circle High School, and directed by Miss Susan Squires, will be presented Thursday, December 20th, at 8:00 a.m. in the Circle High School Auditorium.

The 22-member cast is comprised of students from each class, and an 8-member choir will sing Christmas carols.

The program is a series of several different Christmas stories and poems, some of which are done in the Reader's Theatre style—that is, with the actors carrying the scripts and reading their parts. The program has something everyone will enjoy, so be sure to come.

Admission is free, and coffee, cookies, and candies will be served by the Home Economics girls afterward.

Circle Banner, December 20, 1973

An Old-Fashioned Christmas in Polson, 1975

During the 1970s, some Montana communities sought to reinstitute older traditions during the Christmas season. Occasionally tied to business promotions, these activities focused on the town's children—as they should. In 1975 Polson—the county seat of Lake County—successfully orchestrated such an "old-fashioned Christmas."

*I*T WAS nostalgia personified.

Santa waved to the huddled crowd and a host of children from aboard an ancient stagecoach borrowed from the museum. The matched Belgians labored in their harnesses, blowing steam from their nostrils. Steel shoes splintered the ice beneath two tons of horse flesh, and the rusty wheel rims crunched through the crusted snow.

Small eyes glistened and cheeks reddened as tiny children braved the raw wind from atop dads' shoulders as the makings of their dreams paraded past.

Polson's Old Fashioned Christmas brought out young and old on foot and horseback to share in the holiday festivities.

Cowkids and elk proclaimed "Greetings from Montana" on this western Christmas postcard. Montana Historical Society Photograph Archives, Helena

The parade, a lot shorter than most, progressed on schedule and without delay, perhaps hastened by the bitter winter air.

Shoppers found hotdogs (priced like in the old days at 10 cents each) a practical way to fill empty stomachs. The Retail Trade Committee, which sponsored the sale, bunned up more than 1,600 hotdogs in five hours to hungry shoppers.

Children flocked from the free movie to fill a horse-drawn wagon that provided rides throughout the day. Those riding their own mounts to town tethered them at the livery stable in a vacant lot downtown while they shopped.

And, while there was a mixture of the old-fashioned and the new-fangled seen about in the air, there was a timeless spirit throughout the day. A holiday spirit of fun and good times.

Missoula Missoulian, December 24, 1975

Browning Tribute, 1976

In the summer of 1976, Glenn Heavy Runner, a 14-year-old Blackfeet boy, drowned in a swimming hole near Browning on the Blackfeet Indian Reservation. In his memory, his family lobbied diligently for the construction of a swimming pool in the town so local children would have a safe place to swim. Word of their success came during the holiday season of 1976.

CHRISTMAS WAS CELEBRATED twice at the home of Mr. and Mrs. Eugene Heavy Runner and was enriched with the knowledge that Browning is to have a swimming pool, and with the commemoration of the drowning of Glenn, 14, who drowned at the "75-Cent Hole" last summer. Christmas was celebrated December 25 as well as January 2.

Mrs. Gertrude Heavy Runner, Glenn's mother, said, "Tears of joy flooded my eyes when I learned that the funding was approved for the swimming pool." . . .

"Christ was born into the world to die for all of us so we can be united with God after we die. Glenn died too to bring happiness to all the children so they might enjoy a swimming pool and be safe from drowning."

Tribute was paid to Glenn Heavy Runner on Christmas by the family with the laying of a wreath of red roses on his grave and a 9 a.m. mass. A wooden cross, made by Dwight No Runner, also was placed at the grave.

A shrine was set in the living room of the Heavy Runner home. His picture, his Bible—received in religious education from teacher Robert Bremner—and the sacred heart were placed beside a nativity set. His candle, lighted for him each day, was placed with them among pine tree limbs. . . .

Mrs. Heavy Runner is grateful to all who helped to bring the swimming pool to fruition.

Browning Glacier Reporter, January 6, 1977

Christmas Traditions—Turkey or Fry Bread, 1977

In 1977 Florence Standing Rock related the history of the Christmas holidays on the Rocky Boy's Reservation, revealing how its residents had gradually adopted and adapted the white people's holiday. This Indian reserve was established in 1916 for landless Chippewa and Cree bands. It is located about 20 miles southwest of Havre, primarily in Hill County.

CHRISTMAS IN MONTANA may mean turkey and all the fixin's. Or it could mean fried bread or rose hips if one lives on one of the state's seven Indian reservations. Our ethnic heritage might bring pastries and saffron cake for Cornish descendants in Butte. Or it could be lefsa and lingon berries for the many Scandinavians in the Big Sky Country.

Florence Standing Rock, pioneer on the Rocky Boy Indian Reservation, told her memories of Christmas to Robert C. Lucke, a Havre native and historian. She is the granddaughter of Little Bear, one of two historic chiefs on the Rocky Boy:

It was in 1916 that the band of landless Indians finally found shelter with creation of the reservation. Then, the main winter holiday was New Year's. It was a time to make friends with an enemy, to feast in the teepees—later the tents or cabins. Visiting is still a tradition for the holidays.

Christmas celebrations began to grow with the advent of a Lutheran missionary, Pastor Elmer Burroughs. He had Christmas programs in the old round log hall at the Agency. Gifts were given, a new tradition for the tribe. It was an exciting time because everything was so new—the idea of the birth of Christ as a holiday time.

Menus varied with the times. When it had been a good year, the Indian people ate holiday fare like the white man. In hard times—and they were frequent—chicken and rabbit were sometimes substituted for turkey. Always there was much traditional Indian food prepared with the turkey. Rose hips were formed into patties and fried. Chokeberries and other wild berries, which had been dried, were ground and prepared. Sometimes the berry was a foundation for pemmican. Indian fry bread—dough fried in hot grease— also graced reservation tables.

It was the same with gift-giving. If there was money, candy, toys, and fruit were purchased for the children. Other times, toys were handmade.

Snow-draped evergreens in Upper Geyser Basin, Yellowstone National Park, 1887. F. Jay Haynes, photographer, Haynes Foundation Collection, Montana Historical Society Photograph Archives, Helena

The greatest gift of all was a horse, the highest honor to a friend or relative. Nothing brought more excitement for the family than to have a new horse in the herd. That holds true today.

Another tradition is still followed, with Christmas and New Year's dances.

Not infrequently, the family would give a feast for a loved one who had died.

Perhaps the Rocky Boy people may even think of three "wise men" of their own—three Montanans who fought to get the reservation for these homeless ones. They were Charles M. Russell, the artist; William M. Bole, Great Falls *Tribune* editor; and Frank B. Linderman of Helena and Kalispell, author and insurance man.

Browning Glacier Reporter, December 22, 1977

Polson Christmas Memories, 1977

In 1977 the Flathead Courier in Polson sponsored a contest for its readers to relate their Christmas memories. The winning entries addressed "the magic of Christmas in childhood," including the piece by Barbara Jacques of Polson. Her entry, titled "My Most Memorable Christmas," illustrates one aspect of every Montanan's Christmas: a look at the present in the context of the past.

*W*HEN I THINK of my "most memorable Christmas," my mind readily reverts to my childhood, when my parents turned Christmas into a fantasyland for my sister and me.

On Christmas Eve, save for a few Christmas decorations, our living room looked as normal as any other day. We'd hang our stockings, leave cookies and milk for Santa and carrots for his reindeer, and Mom would read us "The Night Before Christmas." Then we were off to sleep, surely with visions of sugar plums and good things to come dancing in our dreams.

When we awoke, we were to wake our parents before even looking downstairs to the living room. Dad would flip the magical switch at the top of the stairs, and the tree lights would go on, lights would light in all the houses on the train platform, and the train would choo-choo through the tiny village under the tree. In front of the tree and train platform would be all the presents Santa had left. It was truly a sight to behold!

Soon my mother would start the turkey dinner, and then my grandparents and aunt and uncle would come to join us. They were perfect Christmases.

It was not until years later, with young children of my own, that I truly realized the efforts of my parents who trimmed the tree and set up the trains and platform after we were asleep, often only getting an hour or two of sleep. They didn't even forget to leave crumbs from Santa's cookies and reindeer's carrot munchings on the plate we left, definitely proving that our bearded friend had been there.

I am now 3,000 miles from my family, with children and a family of my own. I try to maintain some of the fantasy for my children, but I must admit to lacking my parents' stamina for the all-night Christmas preparations. It's been nine years since I've been with my parents at Christmas, and this is a very nostalgic season for me. I always remember those early Christmases with delight and great gratitude toward my parents, who went to such lengths to give me such beautiful memories.

Polson Flathead Courier, December 22, 1977

Forsyth Decorates, 1979

By the 1970s, most Montana communities were deeply involved in the decoration of business and residential exteriors for the holiday season. In 1979 the simple, tasteful displays won the prizes in Forsyth.

*I*F YOU WERE driving around Forsyth before Christmas, you probably noticed that the neighborhoods were lit up a little bit more this year than in previous years. At least the judges in the Forsyth Business and Professional Women's Christmas decorating contest noted this difference in their annual inspection of the best decorated homes in the community.

The results of the contest showed that the $35 in prize money was being shared among Rev. and Mrs. Conrad Lindeman, Mr. and Mrs. Mort Barrus, and Mrs. Reuben Wilhelm.

The prize for the best overall decorations was awarded to Rev. and Mrs. Conrad Lindeman for their home at 1416 Cedar Street. Despite the theft of a spotlight from the display, the nativity scene showed the beauty of the season.

Mr. and Mrs. Mort Barrus used an ample quantity of lights to decorate the tall pines and shrubbery in front of their house at 587 Oak Street to win the best-decorated-yard category.

The Christmas tree in the living room of Mrs. Reuben Wilhelm at 274 N. Third Avenue was framed in the house's lighted picture window and reflected in a mirror to win the best window award in the BPW contest.

There was also a commercial category in this year's BPW contest. Top prize went to the window of the First Montana Title Company at 879 Main Street. However, there was no prize money awarded in the commercial division.

Forsyth Independent, December 27, 1979

A Wibaux Christmas Story, 1980

In 1980 the *Wibaux Pioneer-Gazette* collected handwritten Christmas stories from the fifth-grade students at the Wibaux Elementary School. This small agricultural community is the county seat of Wibaux County, in extreme eastern Montana.

While several of the Christmas stories are noteworthy, eleven-year-old Richard Jendro's piece, called "Santa's Gone," is a special blend of adolescent imagination and Montana roots. (Richard receives only a B-minus for his spelling!)

*I*T IS THE morning of Christmas and Jerry went out to see his presents. There were no presents ther. Jerry said, "Santa must have got lost last night. I'm going to see if Richard has any presents." Jerry went over to Richard's house. Richard didn't have any presents ether. So Jerry and Richard went out to look. Richard took the thrie wheeler and Jerry took the motercycle.

We found Santa Claus over on Jendro ranch in Dawsan county. Santa had hit a hill. They saw him at the bottom of the hill. Santa was unconshinch. Jerry and Richard hurried back to Richard's place and got the pickup. They went back to the ranch and put the raindeer in the back of the pickup and put Santa in the front. They took Santa to a hospital in Glendive.

When he whook up, they told Santa he was at the hospital and that his raindeer were ok. Then they told him he hit a hill over at our ranch. Santa said Christmas is going to be called off for a few days. Jerry and Richard put it in all the papers in the world that Christmas will be on January 8th this year. All those days in between there, Santa's raindeer were ready.

Well, tonight is Christmas, and Santa is all ready. He left at exzactly 11:30 so he could go to peaples houses. At last he came to Richard's house. He gave Richard a new minicher Corvett and he gave Jerry a minicher pickup.

Wibaux Pioneer-Gazette, December 25, 1980

Helena Christmas Letter, 1980

In 1980 the *Helena Independent-Record,* located in the state capital, solicited letters about Christmas from its readers. The paper published the responses in a special section on Christmas Day. The writing of twelve-year-old Stacey Hargesheimer proves particularly timely and insightful.

*F*IRST, I THOUGHT my Christmases were just regular, but now I know differently.

I guess I'm really lucky. I have three sets of relatives, and every kid knows what that means! Presents! But that's not all. I'm lucky enough to have grandparents who live in Helena, so on Christmas Eve, we can go over to their nice, cozy house, which smells of apple pie and turkey.

And the great big tree with little ornaments that have my brother's and my name on them. And usually I have two places to spend Christmas. This year, I get to go to Minnesota, because I have two dads and a mom.

Also, I've decided that I would rather not be an only child, especially around Christmas. I usually wake up first, before my brother. I go through my stocking which is always on our beds for when we wake up in the morning (which is at 6 or 7). Then I sneak into my brother's room and scream, "Josh!

Wake up! It's Christmas, remember!" If I can't get him up, then our two cats will! And speaking of the cats, sometimes I think they have more fun than I do!

Running around under all the wrapping paper, getting their pictures taken, sitting by the fire, climbing the tree. Ya' know, just thinking about the cats having fun, I know I'm one of the luckiest kids in the world!

Helena Independent-Record, December 25, 1980

Helena's "Secret Santa," 1981

Beginning in 1980, an anonymous donor in Helena provided money for poor families to purchase Christmas gifts for their children. Between 1980 and 1985, this private citizen worked through a local welfare office—asking no questions of the needy applicants except how many children each had. The project grew, and Helena's "Secret Santa" annually gave increased amounts: $35,000 (1980); $40,000 (1981); $46,000 (1982); $50,000 (1983); $56,000 (1984); $78,000 (1985). Tens of thousands of children benefited from his generosity. With the Christmas of 1986, the still-anonymous donor began working through the more formal network of local welfare organizations.

*H*UNDREDS OF CHILDREN will enjoy a happier Christmas this year because an anonymous Helenan has donated about $38,000 to kids who otherwise would have found little if anything under their trees.

Jill Kennedy, head of the Friendship Center at 1503 Gallatin, said the man asked her to place ads offering the money and including the phrase: "God loves all the little children."

The donor wanted to be sure nobody would be left out. He's been in constant touch with the Center to be sure it doesn't run out of money, and he raised the ante three times since the giveaway began Monday morning.

Kennedy said the response was overwhelming.

The Center, normally a low-budget service offering an emergency place to stay and food and clothing to down-and-out families, began writing checks to parents at the rate of up to $20 per child, depending on family size. This morning, after spending $21,360 the first two days, the Center limited further gifts to $50 a family.

Kennedy said the donor specified that there were to be no forms to fill out—there were to be no questions asked except how many children needed gifts. But she was confident that most of the recipients have been truly in need. Apparently nobody who showed up was turned away without money.

Some apparently were in need of a drink. One Helena bartender said that in one day he cashed about $320 worth of Friendship Center checks.

But workers at the Center are sure most of the money was spent for presents for children.

Some people wept as they accepted their checks. One of them said her husband had been unemployed for nine months and that there was no way her children could have had much of a Christmas without the gift.

Linda Erickson of the Center's staff said one family returned with a little gift-wrapped package for the unknown donor—the "Secret Santa"—and pictures of their children.

And while some people stood with tears in their eyes, others were on the phone to their friends: "Get over here! It's for real!"

By late Tuesday morning nearly 300 checks, totaling about $12,000 had been written. By the end of the day, the number of checks reached 396.

At 8 a.m. this morning, a long line of people greeted Center workers. And the check-writing continued.

By noon, 530 families had received checks that added up to $27,300. . . .

Tallon said checks were averaging a little over $50. At three or four children per check, that's something like 2,000 Helena youngsters if all the money were to go for presents.

But as they crawl into bed Christmas Eve, those kids probably aren't worried about whether some people might have abused the donor's generosity.

They, and their parents, just know they'll have a more sparkling Christmas because somebody out there cares about the little children.

Helena Independent-Record, December 24, 1981

St. Nicholas Visits an Oilman

The *Montana Oil Journal* was a trade paper for oilmen first published in 1921. It featured news of the Williston Basin petroleum industry, operating in both Montana and North Dakota. During the Christmas season of 1982, the Journal carried a parody written by John Fitton of the Seahawk Oil Company. In this piece, Santa Claus (not surprisingly) assumed the role of the oilman.

'Twas the plight before Christmas and all through my home,
Not a checkbook would balance—the money was gone.
The bills were all stashed in a corner with care,
In hopes that some royalties soon would be there.
The children were nestled in front of the tree,
While visions of toyland poured forth on TV.
And Sis with her Carte Blanche and Ma with her Master's
Had just left the garage for a shopping disaster.

When out on the lawn there arose such a clatter
I sprang from my desk to see what was the matter.
The sun on the breast of the newly mowed grass
Showed something amazing was coming to pass.
And what should my wondering eyes there enfill
But a little recorder and six tiny drills,
And a little permit-man, so lively and funny.
That I signed on the line without shothole money.

More rapid than eagles those drills did they dig,
And I knew in a moment they'd found something big.
Now Mobil and SoCal and Seahawk and Exxon,
Then Getty and Oxy and Arco and Union,
All came to my door with a lease in their hand—
But I quietly told them to get off my land.

Like dry leaves in a hurricane, I knew for a fact
That the scent of this big one would soon have them back.

And then in a twinkling I heard at the door
The rap of the man whom I waited for.
He glistened with diamonds and so did his car.
But his boots were all tarnished with oil and tar.
The beard on his chin was as white as the snow.
He looked like a jolly old fellow I know.

A sack full of money he had on his shoulder,
In his fist, a gold nugget as big as a boulder.
He said all was mine, plus a certain percent,
If he could drill one hole in my Creeping Bent.

A wink of his eye and a bottle of cheer
Soon gave me to know I had nothing to fear.
He spoke not a word, but went straight to his work.
Up went the derrick, the pipe down with a jerk.

Soon laying a finger aside of his nose,
He stepped back, and straight up the oil it rose.
It encircled his head, like a wreath, black and smelly.
He laughed and he shook like a bowl full of jelly.
He sprang to his car and, before I could see,
He'd erected a bright, shiny, new Christmas tree.
With a wave of his hand and a soft little whistle,
Away went my friend like the down of a thistle.

My worries were over. I sat back in my chair.
Then I thought of the oilmen drilling out there.
"Merry Christmas," I shouted—I'll send them this card.
With the hopes that next year they'll find oil in *their* yard!

John Fitton,
Billings Montana Oil Journal,
December 16, 1982

Ekalaka Prepares for Christmas, 1982

In Montana's smaller communities—like Ekalaka (population 620), the county seat of Carter County in southeastern Montana—the Christmas season is still marked by events that involve most of the townspeople. These are the community activities that survive the years and become local traditions.

*T*HE LIONS CLUB had a very successful "Santa Under the Tree" and movie last Thursday, December 16.

Santa arrived in a horse-drawn chariot complete with sleigh bells, contributed by Bob Strub, and "Ho-Ho-Ho-ing" made his way through quite a gang of kids.

The movie was "Herbie," starring the famous Volkswagon. The grade-school gym was overflowing with cheering youngsters.

Many thanks from the Lions Club to all the businesses for contributing for the sacked candy. The Lions Club sponsored the movie. Thanks to Bob Strub for his horse-drawn chariot, and Castleberrys for the sleigh bells.

Ekalaka Eagle, December 24, 1982

Townsend Christmas Spirit, 1983

More than any other holiday, Christmas is a time for children—and for giving and receiving presents. All too frequently parents are shocked and dismayed by evidence of blatant greed in their children. And occasionally those parents are surprised and rewarded when a child reminds them of the real "spirit of Christmas."

*C*HRISTMAS TIME is here and with it is the excitement in every child as he or she dreams of the many wonderful presents they will receive. Many times they are so caught up in the excitement they forget the meaning of Christmas.

One child who hasn't is Becky Cheever, daughter of Mr. and Mrs. Joe Cheever, Townsend. Recently, Becky wrote to Santa Claus. But after reading several letters to Santa, all asking for their favorite toy, Becky decided to send him a present. Becky and her brother and sisters decided to send $2 to Santa so he could buy himself a present. We are sure he was very pleased to receive Becky's letter.

Townsend Star, December 23, 1983

Christmas Editorial from the High Line, 1983

In December of 1897, eight-year-old Virginia O'Hanlon wrote a letter to the editor of the *New York Sun*. She asked, "Please tell me the truth. Is there a Santa Claus?" Editor Francis P. Church then penned his famous response: "Yes, Virginia, there is a Santa Claus. . . ."

In 1983 Mariann Sutton, editor of the *Phillips County News* in Malta, took this exchange of letters as the inspiration for her Christmas editorial.

*T*HE TWO LETTERS between Virginia O'Hanlon and Francis P. Church were first published 96 years ago. Today they seem quaint relics of an earlier, simpler age—when children still believed in fairies and their fathers still believed in newspapers.

So much has happened in the intervening years to dispel faith in anything. Two world wars, the rise and fall and rise of dictatorships, revolutions, mass murders, the use of nuclear power for destruction, the use of almost any sort of power for destruction, even the attempted assassination of a pope. Through all of this, through the absolute rending of the social fabric of a country and a culture, how can we say that the values that Francis Church cited still survive? Where do you go to find Santa Claus in this day and age?

The answer, of course, is that you go where you have always gone for those values—to the human heart. "He exists as certainly as love and generosity and devotion exist. . . ." The values embodied by Santa Claus, by Christmas, by all that Christians see in the birth of Christ, are those simple, abiding values found within each human heart. They are love, generosity, devotion, compassion, mercy, tolerance—all those finer feelings manifested in the spirit of giving.

Sure, we can warp that spirit, twisting it to our own material ends. So often you hear the lament, "Christmas is too commercial. It means spending money in stores to give things that don't benefit either the giver or the receiver. Why should I do that?"

Well, why should you? I wouldn't want to. If you ask me, that's not too Christmasy.

The giving that we do at Christmas should be giving from the heart, giving because we truly want to make someone else feel good and make ourselves feel better in the process. Giving because you think you must—because of social obligations or in answer to trumpeting advertisements—won't make you feel better. Giving from the heart, because you want to, will. The quality of mercy is not strained, and neither should the quality of giving be forced.

And neither should it be limited.

Think of Christmas as a rehearsal for the giving you might do throughout the year. Love, generosity, and devotion shouldn't be limited to one season or to one small circle of friends and family. The generosity that we show when we contribute to a worthy cause, be it a national fund drive or a hat-passing to help a burned-out neighbor, is as much a part of the spirit of Christmas as the Salvation Army's red kettle on the street corner. The willingness we have to help others around December 25 isn't necessarily tied to the calendar and the clock. These are universal values, timeless traits that prove how much greater than our humanity our human spirit can be.

This is 1983. For some it has been a good year, and for some it has been a bad one. But Virginia O'Hanlon is still with us. Santa Claus will be too, as long as we make sure he continues to exist in our hearts.

So give old Santa a helping hand. Take him with you this summer, when temperatures are high and tempers are short. Remember him when you're thinking of that smart, get-even remark that you'd just love to make. Think of him when you want to spurn an outstretched hand.

Santa is only going to hang around as long as we give him a place to stay in our hearts.

Try to keep the rent as low as possible.

Malta Phillips County News, December 14, 1983

Red Lodge Pageant, 1984

For years Red Lodge has held a "Festival of Nations" to honor its ethnic heritage. Yet the townspeople also can adapt to more recent Christmas events, like "The Best Christmas Pageant Ever."

*A*NYBODY WHO has ever been in a pageant, which probably covers just about anybody who has ever been a child, surely will identify with the antics and poignancy of the holiday production "The Best Christmas Pageant Ever," to be held this weekend at the Roman Theatre. Show times are Friday, December 21 at 7 p.m. and Saturday at 2 p.m. and 7 p.m.

Of the 36-member cast, 30 are children. The offering tells the story of the hellion Herdman children who wreak havoc on a traditional children's

Snow cornice—Beartooth Mts. near Twin Lakes. F. W. Byerly, photographer, Montana Historical Society Photograph Archives, Helena

church Christmas pageant. The undisciplined Herdmans terrorize their fellow classmates by stealing and destroying other children's property, setting fire to a neighbor's tool house, lying, and smoking cigars.

Other children escaped them by going to church until the Herdmans, seeking free cookies given at Sunday School, turn the usually lackluster Christmas pageant into a madhouse.

A television version of the play by Barbara Robinson was broadcast for the third year by ABC last weekend. The director of the local production is Mary Beth Glantz of Red Lodge.

"The Best Christmas Pageant Ever" is not just the story of a church putting together its Christmas play. It's a story of children and adults learning to accept and respect each other in an age where commercialism has taken over our celebrations. It speaks the true meaning of love.

Red Lodge Beartooth Weekly, December 19, 1984

Christmas Energy Gifts, 1984

Just about the time you think there is no new way to secularize and commercialize Christmas, a serious contender comes along. Although based on a valid need, this is Christmas giving gone "cute."

*L*AST-MINUTE Christmas shoppers might want to consider a gift to warm the hearts of recipients—Montana Power's "Gift of Energy" certificates.

Available at all MPC offices, the new gift certificates may be purchased for any amount. The amount then is applied toward the utility bill of the recipient, who receives a "Gift of Energy" certificate for the amount credited on the utility bill.

The certificates will be offered throughout the year by Montana Power, which suggests that they might be appropriate for presents at anniversaries, birthdays, and other holidays. . . .

Glasgow Courier, December 20, 1984

Santa Express Goes to Glasgow, 1984

The long-heard charge that "Christmas has become too commercialized" echoed through the 1980s. Yet, in Valley County on the High Line, an idea that originated among Glasgow businessmen to increase holiday sales quickly became a warm community activity during the Christmas season.

*T*HE SANTA EXPRESS will be on the road early Saturday to pick up residents from all over the county for a free trip to Glasgow.

Points of departure in all of the towns are the schools. The first run is scheduled to leave Opheim at 8:30 a.m., arriving at Glasgow at 9:30 a.m. and leaving Glasgow for Opheim at 2:25 p.m.

For residents in west Valley County, the bus will be ready to load at Saco at 10:35 a.m. and at Hinsdale at 11:15 a.m. The bus will leave Glasgow at 5 p.m. for the return trip.

The Nashua and Fort Peck run is scheduled to leave Nashua at 12:45 p.m. and Fort Peck at 1:30 p.m. Residents from these areas will board the bus at 5:30 p.m. to return home.

Sandy Meeve, chairman of the project, will serve as hostess on the buses coming into Glasgow, and a drawing will be held for a $25 gift certificate on each of the three bus runs. Jeff Hayward will serve as host on the homeward-bound buses.

Persons from the outlying areas may sign up for a seat on the bus by calling Jean Dreikosen evenings, 364-2376, Hinsdale area; Diane Menge, Saco City Office; Bonnie Cherney, Miller Drug, Nashua; George Nicholas, Fort Peck Cafe, Fort Peck; Ernie Jean, Opheim School, Opheim.

"If you want to be assured of a seat, be sure and sign up, but if you are not signed up, come anyway to the school," Meeve said.

Johnnie Holding, school-bus driver, will be driving the Chamber of Commerce bus, with Glasgow businesses picking up the tab for gas and the driver.

"All three towns have ball games that night, and you will all be home in plenty of time to attend the games," Meeve said.

In Glasgow, the Elks Lodge will serve as headquarters, where Rosalie Palazzo will be the hostess. Diana Hanson is assistant hostess. Free refreshments will be served at the Elks, and shoppers riding the bus may check packages there.

If persons want to shop in the outlying areas of the city, a limousine service will be provided under the direction of Becky Erickson. Ron Gore made all of the signs for the special event.

Special invitations have been mailed out to residents of the outlying area.

Glasgow Courier, December 13, 1984

Christmas in Butte, America, 1987

In the early 1980s, the Atlantic Richfield Company (ARCO) closed down the old Anaconda Copper Mining Company properties in Montana. Entire communities were devastated—particularly Black Eagle, Anaconda, and Butte. But the people of Butte fought back. And, by the Christmas of 1987, the *Montana Standard* could boast of "A Full Stocking in Butte, America."

*T*HERE'S SNOW on the ground this Christmas, and the temperature is close to nippy, but the season is enough to warm the cockles of a Butte resident's heart.

Good things are happening in Butte, and folks are looking ahead with optimism and confidence.

Montana Resources Inc. had a good year, and its employees shared in it. MRI's bonuses just before Christmas undoubtedly spread some good cheer throughout the city.

For the first time in decades, Butte has become home to two mining companies. New Butte Mining Inc. has set up shop and is carefully gearing up for larger operations.

The renewed mining activity may be obscuring another development, at least in the minds of people from other parts of the state. We're talking about Butte's growing reputation as Montana's leading city in science and technology. Energy research and ceramics technology are two fields in which Butte is making a name for itself.

Montanans have always been aware of the academic excellence of Montana Tech, but it was still nice to see *U.S. News and World Report*'s poll on colleges nation-wide. College presidents around the country rated Tech No. 1 among the nation's small technical colleges. If quality is what the state's regents and legislators want to see in the University system, Tech will have their support.

Butte also came up the winner in the nip-and-tuck competition for the state-supported transloading facility.

Having both east-west and north-south rail service helped a lot on that, a fact overlooked by a few sore losers.

Butte isn't all business, though. It's also fun. The new High Altitude Sports Center, which sprang into being almost overnight, is a good example of Butte's attitude toward sports and athletic competition, and also an example of its ability to turn a "far-fetched" idea into reality.

Chief Executive Don Peoples and the members of the council of commissioners continue to get the most out of the city's existing revenues, without a lot of complaining about the fact that sometimes government has to tighten its belt along with the taxpayers. That's a refreshing attitude not always visible among the state's public officials. But there's some good news on this front even for the local government: the tax base is gradually broadening.

There are more, but those are some of the tangible blessings Butte can count this Christmas.

Butte Montana Standard, December 25, 1987

Christmas in the Hutterite Colony at Fords Creek, 1989

The Fords Creek Colony is located outside Grass Range in Fergus County. Of the more than three dozen Hutterite agricultural communities in Montana, it is one of the smallest and newer colonies. The "colony boss" at Fords Creek is Martin Stahl, and he is responsible for all of the community's financial and business transactions. Mr. Stahl's youngest daughter, Barbra Joy Stahl Pelan was born on December 20, 1968—so the Christmas celebration on the colony holds special meaning for her. In this piece, Ms. Pelan graciously describes Christmas on the Fords Creek Colony.

Of life on a Hutterite colony, Ms. Pelan also has written: "The Hutterite life is a good life but, like life anyplace else, it is only good because we are satisfied with who we are personally, and that satisfaction reflects on the way we live our everyday lives. It takes a lot of hard work and sacrifice to live in a close community, as we do, with people of different ideas and personalities. You learn to think of your neighbor even before you think of yourself—which is, after all, what God wants us all to do."

Ms. Pelan's comments stand as their own Christmas message.

*C*HRISTMAS IS to us a religious holiday that emphasizes the true meaning of Christmas by centering around the celebration of the birth of Christ. It is also a time for family, and sharing, and gifts, and, of course, food. We do a lot of cooking and baking—Christmas cookies, fruitcakes, and more.

Our Christmas gift from the colony is what we call "nichlos." It is a large assortment of candy, cookies, nuts, fruits, juices, crackers, chips, and soups. The colony boss buys this about two weeks before Christmas, and it is equally divided among the families to munch on during the holidays.

The pre-Christmas preparations of buying or making gifts for loved ones is the same for us as it is everywhere else.

The school children on the colony usually have a Christmas program. It includes plays, the nativity scene acted out, the singing of carols, and the serving of snacks and refreshments. On this occasion, colony members and neighbors gather to socialize in the Christmas spirit.

Christmas Eve is a gathering of the immediate family and an exchanging of gifts, in remembrance of the Three Wise Men who brought gifts to Jesus. We sing Christmas carols and our traditional German Christmas hymns. This is the time when the "nichlos" is really tested out. Some of us do have Christmas trees, and the children believe in Santa Claus—but we try to keep the real meaning of Christmas on the right track, since Jesus is a very important part of our everyday life.

On the morning of Christmas and of the following two days, we have church services that last about an hour and a half. We sing our Christmas hymns, and our sermons pertain to the birth of Christ and to the coming of the Wise Men and the shepherds. It is the same every year, but there is always something new to hear in the sermons.

We have the traditional Christmas Day dinner, with stuffed turkey or goose, and with all the trimmings. We also have special little buns that come from a secret Hutterite recipe, and we have dessert.

On Christmas Day the children have Sunday School in the afternoon. Here they recite German Christmas hymns learned by heart. The Sunday School teacher then gives each child a special package of assorted candy, gum, and fruit as a reward for being a good student. This is a special little tradition that means a lot to the kids.

Each family on the colony does things a little differently, like the families all over the world. Christmas means many things, and we all have our traditions, but we all have one thing in common: the most important thing about Christmas is that Christian worship which emphasizes the true meaning of the holiday and the opportunity to share that celebration with your family and friends.

Courtesy Barbie Stahl Pelan

Elliston and Avon Traditions, 1985

The small communities of Elliston and Avon are located on U.S. Highway 12, west of Helena about twenty-five miles and thirty-five miles, respectively. The towns sit right on the old Northern Pacific Railroad main line, now a part of the Montana Rail Link network. Here, as in many small Montana settlements, the repetition of Christmas activities bespeaks stability in the face of uncontrollable change.

*Y*OU KNOW a tradition is deep when no one can recall its origins or a time when it didn't exist.

Consider the Christmas traditions in Elliston and Avon, those two towns over the Continental Divide west of Helena that were born more than a century ago during Montana's gold mining heydays and brought to life by the railroad.

Avon Postmaster Delbert Mannix, who was born 67 years ago in nearby

Helena artist Robert F. Morgan drew these carolers for *Montana The Magazine of Western History*, circa 1965. Montana Historical Society Library, Helena

Finn, an old and now abandoned mining town, said he can't remember when Avon didn't carry out the same holiday tradition—the annual Christmas play that the school board has organized for tonight.

"They did it in Finn and Avon and all the towns around this country 67 years ago. The same thing then and the same thing now," Mannix said.

Just down the road from Avon, the people in Elliston held their similar Christmas celebration Wednesday evening.

"As far as I know it's been going on forever," said Susan McKee, one of three teachers at the Elliston School.

The traditions are simple and would have been a fitting theme for a Norman Rockwell illustration: the Christmas play at the local school that becomes a community project. You can almost hear the sleigh bells.

In Elliston, a sign-up sheet had been hanging in Bill and Marilyn Thomas' Elliston Store since Thanksgiving. The store, like the school, is a community focal point. The Thomases usually know who is in town and who is not because they run the town's gasoline concession. A fill-up almost always means a trip out-of-town.

Anyhow, the people of Elliston come into the store and jot down their names and a dollar amount they'll donate to the Christmas cause. The donations go toward the purchase of candy, nuts, and fruit that Santa Claus—who, by the way, has lobbied for a new suit this year—gave to the children and senior citizens after the school performance.

Bob Thompson, born in Elliston in 1917, has never left his hometown. He graduated from Elliston High School and served as the school's janitor for 33 years. He still looks forward to the annual Christmas play at the school. "It was going on when I was born and it's always the same, always exactly the same as when I was a kid."

As in past years, Elliston's school children performed a short Christmas play and everyone sang traditional songs.

Nearly the same program will be acted out in Avon tonight. The children are from a different community, but like its neighbors in Elliston, Avon has long celebrated the holiday season by gathering the entire town together as a family.

In their performances in the Community Club, children will act in skits, recite poems, play in a rhythm band, and re-enact the Nativity. Then Santa will arrive.

"Most everyone in the community comes out for it," said Avon's kindergarten and second-grade teacher Kandis Lane.

"It's a social gathering," said Postmaster Mannix. "The kids get up and recite and sing or dance and they exchange gifts. Everybody goes because everybody likes to have their kids show off a little bit."

Over in Elliston, Bob Thompson said he wouldn't miss the Christmas play on a bet. "You have to go," he said. "It's kind of a tradition.

"You just go, it gets to be a habit and habits are funny things. As you grow older, you're anxious to see all the people in the community get together for something like this. You don't get to see your old friends like you used to.

"I guess that's what traditions are for," he said.

Helena Independent-Record, December 19, 1985

Tribune Readers Recount Their
Christmas Miracles, 2000

In December 2000, editors of the *Great Falls Tribune* asked their readers to share stories of strange and wonderful Christmastime experiences. Three Montana writers responded with especially poignant submissions.

*W*HILE MOOSE HUNTING in southern Montana in 1994, I cut a Christmas tree to take home. When we got home my wife and I put the tree up and decorated it. The following week my brother-in-law passed away. We had taken care of him in his last months.

We were given his remains to take to the VA cemetery in Helena the next day, so we placed his ashes under our Christmas tree. When we got up the next morning, the tree had bloomed the most beautiful red candles all over it. The "candles," as they are called, were growths out of the tip of each branch of the tree.

We took this as a sign that my brother-in-law was saying, "Thank you and God Bless."

—Ronald Krattiger, Great Falls

*O*NCE UPON A TIME at a country school I attended, all the children were busy memorizing Christmas poems and stories. As one girl reached the point in the poem where it said, "When all through the house, not a creature was stirring, not even a mouse"—a gopher had somehow gotten in the building and was standing up right on top of a desk eating crumbs from a child's school lunch.

It was a Christmas miracle!

—Ernest Bendorf, Conrad

*M*Y EXPERIENCE at the After Thanksgiving Day sale at Target was quite the deal. I get to Target about 7:10 a.m. The parking lot is practically full! I maneuver my way to toys in search of the Magic Kingdom. I can't find it, so I get a guy to help, who gets a guy to help him. After checking in his computer, he says, "There isn't any Magic Kingdom in our store."

I say, "You mean you advertise the Magic Kingdom, so I get up at 6:00 a.m., just to find out you're just kidding about the Kingdom?"

His solution is to take my telephone number and name and get back to me on this one.

I buy other things I didn't come in to buy—Lincoln Logs and a Barbie Beetle Car. A man and his wife come up to my cart and say, "Where can we find a Beetle Car?"

I say, "You're too late. They were on these shelves. The ones that are now empty."

Sad faces stare back at me. I give them my Barbie Beetle Car. They're ecstatic, and I'm not sure why I even had the Beetle Car in my cart. The women were just grabbing them all around me, so I guess I got caught up in the Beetle Car frenzy.

Well, I've had just about 20 minutes too much of the "Target Zone," and I head up to the front to check out. Holy bucket, Batman! The lines are humbugs! Well, no big deal. I need the rest.

So I get in line and wait. As I'm waiting, my cell phone rings. It's the Target manager, and he's got my Magic Kingdom and will save it for me.

I say, "I've got a better idea. Just bring it to me at check station 11. I'm still standing in line. He does. We exchange Christmas greetings, and he hurries off.

You might think this would be the end of the "Target Zone" experience, but there is one more footnote. The Magic Kingdom isn't as big and impressive as I had pictured it in my mind, and I'm not sure I will keep it.

Then I hear a voice behind me in the line that says, "Where did you find that Kingdom? We have been looking everywhere for it and couldn't find it. Our little girl would love to have had one for Christmas." And, you got it. I say, "Just have this one."

When next year rolls around, I definitely better get to the After Thanksgiving Sale. It's a definite lesson in "It's better to give than to receive."

—Sheryl Flanagan, Great Falls

Great Falls Tribune, December 24, 2000

Christmas Geography Quiz, 1995

The celebration of the Christmas holidays prompts diverse activities. A 1995 Montana-based Yuletide quiz stretches the mind while invoking the season.

*E*ACH OF THE following phrases provides a clue to the name of a town in Montana. If you score eight or higher, Santa will place a special surprise in your stocking.

1. A supernatural messenger of God whom "we have heard on high:"

   _____.

2. "Get on your knees and: _____."

3. A structure from which Christmas tidings ring forth: _____.

4. A single Christmas tree: _____.

5. The King of Kings may be crowned with this garland: _____.

6. A tree cultivated in the Holy Land for its distinctive fruit: _____

   _____.

7. A tender of livestock at the manger: _____.

8. A geometric figure that sits atop a Christmas tree: _____.

9. An important constellation in the southern hemisphere: _____.

10. The acknowledged "Christmas tree capital of Montana:" _____.

Whitefish Pilot, December 21, 1995

Answers to Quiz:
1. *Angela (Rosebud Co.) 2. Pray (Park) 3. Belfry (Carbon) 4. Lonepine (Sanders) 5. Laurel (Yellowstone) 6. Olive (Powder River) 7. Sheperd (Yellowstone) 8. Silver Star (Madison) 9. Southern Cross (Deer Lodge) 10. Eureka (Lincoln)*

Glasgow Santa Service, 2001

Across Montana, Christmastime prompts an array of seasonal work—from the obvious Christmas-tree and turkey-growing industries to the production of traditional arts and crafts for local markets to some unexpected sidelights. Jim Jensen of Glasgow has developed an expertise that falls into the last category.

*J*IM JENSEN doesn't grow grain or raise cattle. But come Christmastime, the jovial Hi-Line man produces one of Montana's hottest commodities.

Each November, Jensen, 54, farms out his team of 20 Santas to shopping malls across the United States.

The clean-shaven need not apply. Jensen's Santas have the whiskers—and figures—to match the real thing.

"I've got some good lookin' boys, I'll tell you that right now," said Jensen, himself the spitting image of St. Nick.

Started seven years ago, Jensen's "JJ's Santa" business is among the most reputable in the United States. When malls ask photography companies for a Santa with an authentic beard, they call Jensen. Last year he sent a Santa to Hong Kong.

It all started in Vietnam, he says.

Stranded in the war zone for 50 days at a time, Jensen and his Navy buddies experimented with facial hair.

"Just for nothing better to do we'd have a beard contest, and then we'd cut designs in it," he said. "I just kept the mustache."

Jensen's wife and three kids had never seen his upper lip until he shaved one day eight years ago. "When I let my mustache grow back in, I let my beard come in too," Jensen said.

A friend suggested he apply for a Santa job.

Jensen bristled, but he couldn't shake the idea.

His first Santa stint was in Tracy, California.

"The people that got me started did a good job," he said. "I just thought I could do it a little better."

Jensen had just been laid off from his job as a chemical dependency counselor. So he began recruiting.

Jensen holds his Santas to a strict code of conduct, said Jerry Swanson, 71, a merry, retired Presbyterian minister and former school teacher from Wolf Point.

Rule No. 1: Don't lie.

"There are always those who wonder if you're a real Santa," said Swanson, whose sleigh is parked at Ross Park Mall in north Pittsburgh this Christmas. "We just take hold of our beard and yank it and say, 'What do you think?'"

Swanson, a portly man with a prodigious white beard, has been known to finish off his Santa look with a visit to a hair salon. Jensen, who is working in Billings this year, does his own styling.

"I've learned how to use a blow dryer and a curling iron, believe it or not," Jensen said.

So, Santa, what's at the top of this year's wish lists?

Bob the Builder toys and anything Harry Potter, Swanson said. But, he adds, the lists are shorter this season.

"I have some feeling that it has to do with the uneasiness of the world right now, the war on terrorism, the uncertainty of things," Swanson said. "This is the first time we've had so much happen on our own shores."

Swanson's wife Barbara will soon join him in Pittsburgh to ease the holiday away from home. The Santa costume is hot and the shifts long, Swanson admits: 7 a.m. to 8 p.m. Sunday through Thursday and 7 a.m. to 9 p.m. Friday and Saturday.

But Swanson's eyes sparkle when he talks about his winter job.

"I'm a school teacher," he said. "I don't miss the classroom, but I miss the kids, and I think that's why I'm here."

Jensen, too, says his holidays are less about money than making people happy.

Though the Santa service is thriving, it's only part of Jensen's year-round photography business. And his costume stays on after hours, for visits to Billings hospitals and nursing homes.

Last year he brought Yuletide cheer to a 100-year-old woman and gave an hour-and-a-half-old baby her first Christmas present at the birthing center at Deaconess Hospital.

"The thing that makes it all worthwhile is the kids. When you see the twinkle in their eye, things kind of fade away," Jensen said. "This is the best job I've ever had."

Helena Independent-Record, December 2, 2001

Drive-up Santa in Plains, 2000

Christmastime offers the opportunity to honor past traditions while modifying them because of this year's circumstances. That kind of modification rests at the heart of the "drive-up Santa" idea, popularized in the small, western-Montana town of Plains.

*N*o FIGHTING the shopping mall crowds. No long treks through blizzards and over tundra to the North Pole. No last-minute logging on to Santa-dot-com.

Just drive up with the kids and let them talk to Mr. Claus without leaving the car.

It's drive-up Santa at a drive-through outdoor kiosk at the Sanders County Fairgrounds in Plains.

Santa emerges from the little log house near the exit gate of the fairgrounds, hands you and yours some cellophane-wrapped candy canes, and takes your order.

"I want Legos," said Matthew Nance, age 3, bundled up in his red parka and holding his mother's hand.

"I want Barbie," said Charlet Nance, age 2, bundled up in a green parka.

"This is a good idea," said their mother, Raven Nance.

Becky DelGiudice, a Plains Lions Club volunteer, was the Santa on duty for the Friday night shift. Only about 10 cars came by Santa's hut then, plus a few strollers, like the Nance family. It was a slow night, Santa said.

Santa informed us that on the previous Sunday, another Santa had handed out 104 candy canes to drive-by visitors.

Santa-DelGiudice was adorned in a traditional one-size-fits-most, red-and-white Santa suit. She donned a long white beard that covered her face almost to her eyebrows. She wore a big black belt she kept tugging up above her waist, trying to keep Santa's pants from slipping downstairs.

The Santa suit was a loaner from the local post of the Veterans of Foreign Wars, where Santas typically are a little burlier than Becky. They also have more manly voices.

"Kids are expecting a Santa with a much deeper voice," DelGiudice admitted. "One little girl smiled at me and said, 'It's OK. It's Santa's helper.'"

The drive-through Santa is the work of Mike Hashisaki, the Sanders County Fair's part-time manager, and Kim McNeil, the fair's groundskeeper. They began the fairgrounds Christmas display four years ago by stringing some lights on the flagpole and plugging them into an electric socket. Since then, the display has evolved to cover almost the entire fairgrounds. Eight to 10 acres are under lights, Hashisaki estimated.

"In the winter, there's not much going on, and we're sort of bored," he said.

Great Falls Tribune, December 18, 2000

Christmas Tree Glut Arrives, 1990

An important share of business in Montana remains seasonal. A case in point is the state's Christmas-tree industry, which supplies trees to West Coast, Midwest, and southern Great Plains markets. What was a thriving business in the 1980s hit hard times in the early 1990s. It took the remainder of the decade for the Montana industry to stabilize and rebuild.

*T*HE CHRISTMAS-TREE glut that has been predicted for several years has arrived, both nationally and regionally, industry spokesmen in Montana say.

"The Christmas-tree industry on a nationwide basis is over-planted," said Ray Brandewie, former state legislator who is president of the Montana Christmas Tree Association.

"There are an awful lot of trees on the market," agreed Linda McHenry of McHenry Trees and Nursery, secretary of the association. She said

McHenry sold its Christmas-tree operation in 1987 and has concentrated on its nursery and seedling business.

"It sounds exactly like what I've been hearing," said Chuck Keegan, who tracks the forest-products industry for the University of Montana Bureau of Business Research.

Neither the state nor the industry has figures on Christmas-tree sales, but Brandewie estimated 3 million to 5 million Christmas trees are planted in northwestern Montana between Whitefish and St. Ignatius. The industry may be valued at $4 million to $5 million for plantation trees alone, not counting the sale of wild trees, wreaths, and other products.

McHenry said Montana has about 100 growers, about 40 of whom are members of the association.

Established growers generally have been able to keep sales steady, but newcomers have had trouble developing a clientele, Brandewie and McHenry agreed.

"It was a seller's market five or 10 years ago," Brandewie said. "A lot of people put in trees without the foggiest notion of where they would sell them."

As recently as three or four years ago, it was not unusual to have the entire crop sold by September, but now sales may continue into December, he said.

Most Christmas trees are harvested at about seven years, but growers have a two- or a three-year margin before trees become too big to make attractive Christmas trees. Still, western Montana may see some growers cutting and burning leftover trees this spring to make way for new plantings.

Brandewie said the state and national Christmas-tree associations are plunging into marketing, and he hopes Montana can persuade more out-of-state buyers about the virtues of Montana trees.

"We're probably selling 100 percent or 115 percent of the trees we sold in 1986 or 1987," he said, adding that several factors have pruned Montana's share of the market.

"The plastic tree is really our biggest problem," Brandewie said.

The national association is trying to woo back those buyers by arguing that live trees are a renewable resource and help replenish the atmosphere.

Helena Independent-Record, January 25, 1990

Kalispell Hospice Tree of Lights, 1992

Christmastime provides us all the opportunity to reflect on our past successes and losses. One formalization of this reflection is provided in several Montana communities by local Hospice groups. This example appeared as an ad in the Kalispell daily.

*F*LATHEAD HOSPICE invites you to help set the Hospice Tree of Lights aglow in honor of a deceased friend or loved one. The Tree Lighting Ceremony is on Thursday, December 3, 1992. A reception will be held from 6:00 to 6:30 p.m. The ceremony begins promptly at 6:30 p.m. at the Health Promotion Center, 1275 Highway 93 North. A Family Affair—Everyone Welcome!

A single light will be added for each person you wish to remember and that person's name will be inscribed in our Memorial Book. The suggested donation is $10 per light. Make checks payable to Flathead Hospice.

Kalispell Daily Inter Lake,
November 22, 1992

Monarch Couple Enjoys a Quiet Holiday, 2001

One of the welcomed aspects of Christmastime is the repetition of holiday experiences—repetitions that build into traditions. Yet those traditions change year by year, generation by generation. Ms. Carol Holoboff of Monarch shines a humorous light on changing customs in this bittersweet piece.

Martha and Russell Corn with their freshly cut Christmas tree, near Superior, 1988. Dick Roberts, photographer, courtesy Mary Alice Chester

*L*AST YEAR we breathed a sigh of relief as our children and their children, with all of their Christmas loot, drove out of the driveway. Maybe it is time for our children to be home for Christmas, in their own homes.

The traditions and rituals we so carefully nurtured over the years are gradually giving way to a Generation X life style. Each year the menu gets larger and the tree taller, as their father and I try to make this Christmas the best one ever—but each year we enjoy it less. Our children are grown and have changed, and we have grown and stayed the same, as much as we can.

One year our daughter from Oregon, who belongs to some kind of "green" club, confronted her father with his lack of ecological consciousness when he brought in a fresh pine tree from the pasture.

The younger grandchildren know who Santa is and won't bother with letters to the North Pole or visits to the mall with "lists" for the guy with the fake beard. They do make lists, after they visit the mall, and write down the name and bar-code information of the items they want.

Our children no longer go caroling to stop for hot cocoa and cookies at neighbors' homes. The teen grandchildren filled our home with strange music last year. Rock and heavy metal sent our old kitty to the basement for the season.

Winter feeding on the Lind Ranch, Zortman, 1957. Montana Historical Society Photograph Archives, Helena

Our home is not on 34th Street, and we do not expect miracles, just a little respect. MTV's Madonna is not the lady from the manger. Our little girl, who had played Mary in the manger scene at our church Christmas program two years in a row, now rallies against manger scenes that threaten the separation of church and state. She declined an invitation to Midnight Mass and announced that she is an agnostic. I'm not sure what that means—probably something to do with being antagonistic.

One of our boys is a vegetarian and requested Tofurkey. His brother jogged out the door every morning without his bacon and eggs and refused my cookies and fudge. The jolly guy with a pack on his back last year was none other than our college student bringing home his laundry from fall term.

BAH! HUM BUG! "There's no place like home for the holidays." And everyone should stay there!

This year my husband and I will celebrate Christmas our own way. Our pine tree will smell better each day as it gets a little drier. We will bring in the Yule log and sit by the fire in our flannel jammies munching on fudge, while Bing sings about a "White Christmas."

We will tell the stories that belong to the handmade ornaments, and Midnight Mass will remind us of the "holy night" for which we celebrate. We can go to bed before dawn. The stockings have been mailed. With Ma in her kerchief and Pa in his long johns, we will sleep late and open our little treasures while we sip hot eggnog and much on real fruitcake.

We know "It's a Wonderful Life," and we will eagerly accept collect calls from our children of Christmases past—if they call before we go out for dinner.

Great Falls Tribune, December 25, 2001

[*Montana and the New West*]

Troy's Christmas Food Basket Program, 2000

Through time, Montanans have given selflessly at Christmastime both as individuals and as groups. That tradition continues in communities both small and large, frequently with heart-rending results. In the northwestern Montana community of Troy, locals have formalized the job of providing food for the needy through a Christmas food-basket program.

*W*E NEED your help to serve our annual Christmas baskets to hungry, hurting people of the Troy area. Last year the Troy Food Pantry distributed over 120 baskets. As seen below, $19.73 provides a complete Christmas meal to a Troy household that is in need.

Onion	$ .35
Cranberry Sauce	$ .59
Rolls	$1.49
Canned Yams	$1.19
Ham or Turkey	$8.50
Apples-Oranges	$2.00
Potatoes	$ .40
Canned Vegetables	$ .33
Stuffing Mix	$1.09
Pumpkin/Apple Pie	$2.89
Celery	$ .90
TOTAL	$19.73

Non-perishable food goods are also appreciated and may be left in drop baskets at Steins IGA or Kootenai Drug/True Value Hardware. Please mail your tax-deductible donations to: Troy Food Pantry, P.O. Box 945, Troy, Montana 59935.

Troy handbill, December 2000

Great Falls Christmas Recollections, 2000

"Christmases past" form one of the most solid memories for the people of any generation. In these recollections from residents of the Rainbow Retirement Center in Great Falls, the traditions recalled cover a broad spectrum.

*W*E LIVED ON a ranch north of Helena, just west of the Sieben Ranch. We went out and cut our own Christmas trees, but Santa always decorated them for us. We never saw the tree again until it was all decorated on Christmas morning.

We had candles on the tree because it was before the days of electricity in rural areas. We would light the candles for 15 minutes, then we would blow them out because the fire danger was so great—and it made the candles last longer.

We got oranges in our stockings and sometimes a banana, but the only presents we ever got were sent by our aunt in Chicago. It if weren't for her, it wouldn't have been much of a Christmas. This was during the Depression, and we didn't have very much money.

—Margery Robbins, 74

I WAS ONE of five children of immigrant parents. Christmas in the Ukraine was quite different from the festivities here. In the first place, my parents were very poor, and extras like Christmas were hard to come by.

Our mother couldn't seem to get these festivities into her comprehension. So all the Christmas we had, we children did. For instance, we had a desk that, when covered, served as a fireplace really nicely.

Our gifts, as few as we could afford, we took turns opening up. That was a real thrill, as there weren't many. We did have a tree that was much appreciated.

Would that today's children could hear of this sort of Christmas. We always were in a Christmas program at church, helping us remember the real meaning of Christmas.

—Adoline Preputin, 85

Drifter, Sheep Wagon, and Band. Winter Camp. 1907, Miles City area. L. A. Huffman, photographer, Montana Historical Society Photograph Archives, Helena

*M*Y DAD worked on a sheep ranch, so we were pretty much alone at Christmas. We had visions of Christmas trees. And we had a big plate with candy and nuts and cookies left by Santa Claus.

In the early 1920s, we moved to Chinook. I remember going to midnight Mass on a night that was so icy cold that I could see each chimney in Chinook with smoke coming straight out of it.

For Christmas, I usually got a separate little plate with nuts and candy. We also each got one apple, one orange, and one banana.

My mother would sew a new head on my doll, and that was our Christmas present. But we were happy—we didn't know any better.

—Dolly Zini, 86

Great Falls Tribune, December 24, 2000